" The whole world without Art would be one great wilderness.

THE PAINTERS OF BARBIZON

COROT
DAUBIGNY
DUPRÉ

By JOHN W. MOLLETT, B.A.
AUTHOR OF THE LIVES OF " WATTEAU" AND " MEISSONIER " IN THIS SERIES

LONDON
SAMPSON LOW, MARSTON, SEARLE & RIVINGTON
LIMITED
ST. DUNSTAN'S HOUSE, FETTER LANE
1890

Printing Statement:

Due to the very old age and scarcity of this book,
many of the pages may be hard to read due to the
blurring of the original text, possible missing pages,
missing text, dark backgrounds and other issues
beyond our control.

Because this is such an important and rare work, we
believe it is best to reproduce this book regardless of
its original condition.

Thank you for your understanding.

ILLUSTRATED BIOGRAPHIES OF
THE GREAT ARTISTS

THE PAINTERS OF BARBIZON

COROT
DAUBIGNY
DUPRÉ

Illustrated Biographies of the Great Artists.

ADDITIONAL VOLUMES.

Each volume, with about twenty illustrations : bound in cloth.
Price 3s. 6d.

THE PAINTERS OF BARBIZON.* I. Memoirs of JEAN FRANÇOIS MILLET, THEODORE ROUSSEAU and NARCISSE DIAZ. By J. W. MOLLETT, B.A.

THE PAINTERS OF BARBIZON.* II. Memoirs of CAMILLE COROT, CHARLES FRANÇOIS DAUBIGNY and JULES DUPRÉ. By JOHN W. MOLLETT, B.A.

WILLIAM MULREADY, Memorials of. Collected by FREDERIC G. STEPHENS.

DAVID COX and PETER DE WINT. Memoirs of their Lives and Works. By GILBERT R. REDGRAVE. [*In preparation.*]

GEORGE CRUIKSHANK, His Life and Works : including a Memoir by FREDERIC G. STEPHENS, and an Essay on the Genius of GEORGE CRUIKSHANK by W. M. THACKERAY. [*In preparation.*]

THE LANDSCAPE PAINTERS OF HOLLAND : RUISDAEL and HOBBEMA, CUYP and POTTER, and others. By FRANK CUNDALL. [*In preparation.*]

"GAVARNI," Memoirs of. By FRANK MARZIALS. With many Illustrations. [*In preparation.*]

VAN EYCK, MEMLINC, MATSYS, and other Painters of the Early Flemish School. [*In preparation.*]

* The two volumes in one : bound in half morocco : gilt tops. Price 7s. 6d.

[LONDON :
SAMPSON LOW, MARSTON, SEARLE & RIVINGTON,
LIMITED,
ST. DUNSTAN'S HOUSE, FETTER LANE.

PORTRAIT OF COROT. *From a Photograph.*

EDITOR'S PREFACE.

THE great interest that has been excited, not only in Paris, but in all countries in which the fine arts are cultivated, by the works of the painters who are known as the Barbizon School, can be readily gauged by the immense number of books and treatises that have been written concerning them during the past quarter of a century. We can but refer our readers to the condensed Bibliography which has been compiled with some pains and which is given in the Appendix to this and to the companion volume. From the books therein mentioned, and largely from contemporary magazine and newspaper articles, too numerous to recapitulate, has been obtained the information which we now offer to English students, in the hope that even these brief memoirs will give them a useful account of the general significance of the lives and works of the six representative painters selected for study. Mr. D. C. Thomson's important work on the Barbizon School of Painting is on the eve of being published ; and we trust that the exhaustive work on Corot, upon which M. Robaut has been so long engaged, will shortly appear. These two volumes will form a prominent addition to the literature of the Barbizon School.

As many illustrations as were available are given, in order to show the characteristic points of each artist.

April, 1890.

NOTE.—The present volume treats of Corot, Daubigny and Dupré; the companion volume of Millet, Rousseau and Diaz.

PAGE

DAUBIGNY—

VII. Special Bibliography 112
VIII. Principal Pictures and their Owners . . . 113
IX. Original Etchings 115
X. Etchings after Pictures by him 116

DUPRÉ—

XI. Special Bibliography 116
XII. Principal Pictures and their Owners . . . 117
XIII. Original Lithographs 119

INDEX.

To Corot 121
To Daubigny 122
To Dupré 124
To Conclusion 125

LIST OF ILLUSTRATIONS.

— ● —

COROT.

Portrait of Corot . . . . From a Photograph. *Frontispiece*

PAGE

The Pond at Ville d'Avray . . . . By Corot. 3

The Banks of the Stream 7

The Lake of Garda 11

The Ruin 12

The Entrance to a Village 14

An Evening in Normandy 20

The Reed Cutter 23

In the Marshes 25

Storm on the Sandhills . . . . . ,, 27

The Dance of the Nymphs 31

Monument to Corot 33

DAUBIGNY.

Portrait of Daubigny . . . . . . By himself. 34

The Flock of Geese . . . . By Daubigny. 39

Shepherd and Shepherdess . . . Etching by Daubigny. 43

The Marsh . . . ., ,, 45

Springtime . . . . By Daubigny. 49

Landscape . . . . ,, 51

On the Oise . . . . ,, 55

xii LIST OF ILLUSTRATIONS.

DUPRÉ.

		PAGE
Coast Scene	By Dupré.	59
The Punt	,,	63
The Pool	,,	71
The Setting Sun	,,	75

NOTE.—During the last ten years, Science has greatly improved many applications of the photographic art, but it has not yet been enabled to reproduce pictures of such intangible qualities as those executed by the Painters of Barbizon with a clearness sufficient to enable the craftsmen of process-blocks to give their best results. This will account for the want of detail apparent in some of the illustrations; which, nevertheless, it is hoped will be found to give characteristic impressions of the works of the several artists.

CAMILLE COROT.

I.

JEAN-BAPTISTE-CAMILLE COROT, landscape-painter, was born at Paris, on the 20th July, 1796, or as it would be called at that time, under the Directory, the year VIII.

His mother was a milliner and dressmaker, very much in vogue, and owned the house in which the painter was born, on the Quai Voltaire, at the corner of the Rue du Bac, and facing the Pont Royal. M. Charles Blanc informs us that about 1846 the old name was still on the wall, in yellow letters on a black ground : "MADAME COROT, MARCHANDE DE MODES."

Corot had two sisters, the elder of whom, Madame Sennegon, was of a feeble constitution, attributable, M. Blanc suggests, to the emotions that her mother suffered during "the Terror," at the date of her birth. She lived, however, to a good old age, in the most affectionate relations with her brother, whose death followed closely on her own. His other sister, Madame Froment, died young, and her dowry, reverting to the family, became the portion of Corot and supplied the modest income which enabled him to follow his chosen pursuit, untroubled with the care of earning his own living. He never married.

His father came of a good old peasant stock from the vine-yards of Burgundy, and he himself was a tall, powerful, rubi-

cund, and above all a kindly and fascinating man—all his life
surrounded by an atmosphere of love and friendship, and in
requital a true lover of his friends, and a self-sacrificing benefactor of those who were in need of his help. He boasted
much of his peasant blood.\ His grandfather's father was a
"cultivator" at a village called Mussy-la-Fosse, near Semur, in
the Côte-d'Or. Corot discovered the existence of some distant cousins in this village, and paid them a visit in 1860, and
wrote home : "The country is full of honest labourers of the
same name as myself—they call out to each other in the fields,
on all sides, 'Hé, Corot!'—one hears nothing else. I thought
they were all calling me, and felt like one of the family."

Corot's father, husband of the "Marchande de Modes," was
a thrifty tradesman, liberal in his way and according to his
lights, but thrifty. He sent the boy, in his tenth year (1806),
to the Lycée at Rouen, on an arrangement *in formâ pauperis* by
which he was received at half price.

But his father had a business friend at Rouen who looked
after the boy, and took him out for walks on his holidays ; and
M. Dumesnil, narrating from recollections of Corot's own
reminiscences, says that this friend, although a kind, was "a
gloomy man, and fond of solitude and of walking in out-of-
the-way places, and in the evening about dusk under big trees
in the meadows, or by the side of the river," and speculates
that the discipline of these mournful holiday walks may have
given the first impulse to the /misty and dream-clad poetry
of the painter's subsequent mood expressed in his art.

Ten years or so later, when Corot must have been already engaged in his artistic studies, his father bought
a country-house at Ville d'Avray, of which we have a
marshy and rheumatic but mist-clad poetical account. "It
was near a *pond*, which has now been filled up, and

THE POND AT VILLE D'AVRAY. BY COROT. *From the Collection of M. Monjean.*

often when the rest of the household were asleep young Corot remained through great part of the night leaning out of window, looking at the sky, and the water, and the trees; and to this habitual contemplation of the watery vapours of the night he himself attributed the readiness with which, when he took up his brush, he remembered the tones proper to express this grey mist, light and floating, with which the air is saturated, and which veils the sky and obscures the horizon in nearly all of his pictures." The explanation is that given by Corot himself of the origin of his own taste for and tendency towards the poetry of landscape.

His first employer was a M. Delalain, who kept a draper's shop in the St. Honoré quarter, and his second in a similar shop in the Rue de Richelieu, "where," M. Charles Blanc tells us, "he began to make drawings under the counter." On the whole, he was in this employment for the eight years of his youth from 1812 until 1820, and attributes to its discipline the excellent habits of order and regularity of which he reaped benefit for the rest of his long and comfortable and honoured life; one of these habits was that of rising early, and punc- tually arriving at his studio "at three minutes before eight in the morning."

It was during his service in the shop in the Rue de Richelieu that he made the acquaintance of the painter, Michallon.

"My first drawing from nature," he said in his old age to his friend M. Réné Ménard, editor of the *Gazette des Beaux-Arts*, "I made at Arcueil, under the eye of Michallon, whose only advice to me was to render with the utmost fidelity everything that I saw before me. His lesson has been useful; it has remained the invariable tendency of my disposition, always inclined to accuracy," which is very pretty *blague*, but, like many estimates of their own qualities by men of genius, *pre-*

cisely the reverse of the truth. In a charming letter to a friend, which we shall revert to, he says with much greater felicity : "Je rêve mon tableau, plus tard je peindrai mon rêve."

"There is a classic element in the pseudo-realism of Corot," says M. Timbal. "How many times, intending to trace the poor outlines of the hills of Ville d'Avray, he has made of it an Arcadian landscape ! How many little white houses hidden away in the foliage he has disguised as antique temples ! "

"Corot, the Schubert of landscape," says M. Fournel, "a classic mollified, and powerfully carried away by Romanticism, mingling on his canvases, in a charming, good-hearted fusion, the lake of Lamartine with that of his master Bertin, recollections of the sacred groves with the groves of Meudon, and drawing from this amalgam the Corot Nature—a nature deliciously impossible, where, in the uncertain twilight of dawn, in the shade and retirement of great trees shrouded in mysteries, we hear the gentle beating of the wings of awakening Love. His pictures always set me thinking of that melody that Paganini played on a single string, but a beautiful note to those who love it; and what a pity it is that we have heard it so often ! Do not listen to the scoffers who will tell you that the fiddle of Corot is only a guitar ! It is really and truly a Straduarius, whose dreamy melodies have set more than one mournful soul a weeping. Wordsworth might have been glad to sing Corot's *Lake of Némi,* and Arcadia been envious of this work in the enchanted forest that he shows us shivering in the hoar frost and the dew of the *Morning.*"

Nothing is more pleasant than the interested, *caressing* tone of all the writings of his friends about their beloved Corot's personal biography, and the pride and affection with which they treasure his gossiping reminiscences of his youth, obviously

one and all feeling the *man* still more endeared to them than
the *artist*, and regarding him still more as a dear old friend
whom it was an honour to be intimate with than as the great
poet of landscape that he was. M. Dumesnil's report of Corot's
own story of his final liberation from trade and commencement
of the study of art is a charming example of this. It was on
a visit that he made to Corot, on 8th December, 1858 (*i.e.*,
Corot would be sixty-two), in the company of Troyon, Français,
and Busson, that he obtained the following details :—

"Corot prayed his father to give him leave to quit commerce and become a painter, for it was what he desired more
than anything in the world. His father reluctantly consented,
and said, 'Your sisters' portions were ready for them to the
minute, and I was hoping soon to provide properly for your
establishment in life, for you are old enough now to stand at
the head of your own house of business ; but since you refuse
to continue the pursuit of your trade for the sake of painting,
I give you notice that in my lifetime you will have no capital
to dispose of. I will give you an annuity of 1,500 livres
(£60 sterling). Never expect anything else, and see if you
can get along with that !'

"And Camille, much moved, embracing his father, cried, 'I
thank you ! It is all I want, and you make me very happy.'

"Almost on the same day, giving himself time for no more
than to buy the necessary tools of an artist, he made his first
study, in the centre of Paris, almost close to the paternal house.
He went down to the tow-path by the Seine, not far from the
Pont Royal, looking towards the city, and full of joy, began to
paint. All who have been admitted to Corot's studio know this
first performance of his brush. He used to show it to us and
say, 'While I was painting *that*, it was thirty-five years ago.
The young girls who worked at my mother's were curious to

see Monsieur Camille at his new work, and they ran away from
the shop to come and look at it. One of them, whom we will
call Mademoiselle Rose, came oftener than the others. She is
living still. She was never married, and she visits me from
time to time; she was here last week.

"'Oh! my friends, what a change! and what thoughts it
starts! My painting has not *budged*. It is as young as ever.
It marks the hour and the time of day when I did it; but
Mademoiselle Rose and I, where are we?'"

Michallon was a young teacher, and Corot studied under him
for only a very short time, but—in so far as it was possible for
the genius of Corot to incur such a debt—Corot owed something, and the world owed something, to Michallon's influence,
congenial with the untaught, spontaneous tendency of his
pupil's natural apprehension of Nature.

"At a time," says M. René Ménard, "when only conven-
tional landscape was known, with the inevitable temple in the
background and the foreground of large leaves as *repoussoir*,
Michallon was regarded as a seeker after Realism, because his
subjects were chosen from Nature instead of being composed
in the imagination."

"A conscientious student of Nature, notable for freshness
and power of colour, but also for mannerism. His foliage and
leaf-work minutely copied," says another critic.

And, with this, it is noteworthy that this young apostle of
the "Renaissance in miniature" began his career in docility to
the Academicians of his day, and was the first recipient, in
1817, of the *Prix de Rome*, then recently founded for landscape.*

* Michallon was the pupil successively of David, Valenciennes, and
Victor Bertin.

THE BANK OF THE STREAM.   BY COROT.   *In the Collection of M. Maurice Gentien.*

Corot told his friend, M. Henri Dumesnil, in after years, that "The precepts that Michallon gave me can be resumed in a few words :/to come face to face with Nature, to endeavour to render Nature with exactness, to paint what one sees, and to translate the impression received." "The advice," M. Dumesnil adds, "was good, and was nearly identical with that which Corot in his turn gave to young people."

Unhappily, Michallon was not permitted to follow his pupil's progress; he died, like Géricault before him, in his youth—only twenty-six years old—and Corot passed into the hands of Victor Bertin, who is mentioned as "the acknowledged chieftain of historical landscape," with whom, according to another critic, "he wasted his time in academical studies." "An excellent draughtsman and an indifferent colourist, but who understood better than anybody else the composition of a landscape." "A pure Classic," M. Dumesnil calls him, "who put everything in its proper order, and whose pictures remind us of the frigidity of the accessories of tragedy." It was not from such a master that Corot would have learned the methods of expression of the delicate and tender side of Nature, which made the poetry and the charm of all his work; these were his already in himself, and were strong enough to resist the influence of Bertin, but he did acquire under Bertin "purity of design, of *charpente* (plan), and composition, which he never lost."

The commentaries of M. Dumesnil, being avowedly the expressions of Corot himself, are the most interesting.

To appreciate the nature of "academical studies" of this precise period it is useful to quote from their own advocates rather than from the writings of their detractors. The essential principle of the classical school appears epigrammatically expressed by the writer of the critical article in the *Moniteur* upon the Salon of the year 1822, and includes the following axioms :—

1. *Modern Schools of Art exist and flourish only by the transmission of the Greek doctrines.*

2. *In the time of paganism the process was from the Form to the Thought, which is favourable to the cultivation of the arts ; whilst now the Thought is applied to animate the Form, which makes us indifferent to the latter.*

The Romantic school of landscape, therefore, of which some say that Paul Huet was the first decided exponent, is fairly qualified as for those "who express their own poetic emotions in the presence of Nature," and Victor Bertin and his pupil Corot appear almost at the two poles of the above antagonism ; and with reference to the transition of public appreciation from the old to the new, through such intermediate men as Géricault, Michallon, Paul Huet, Aligny, and others, there was no sudden shock. "In the limpid and stormless blue," says Charles Clément, " which covered with its pacific canopy the long manifestations of David and his imitators, the clouds rose one by one in the distance, and only by a timid progress drew together and banked up in a style to veil with their tumultuous *cortége* this imposing serenity." Of Corot, as of Géricault, it was true that he was not a Romanticist of *parti pris ;* "it was in allowing himself to be guided naturally by his own feeling for the picturesque that he rebelled against the *decorative, abstract,* and *arid* style'of painting of the First Empire."

He did not, as it were, raise the standard of revolt. On the contrary, his incessant introduction of classical accessories was a permanent tribute of docility towards his first teachers.

"Corot entered on his apprenticeship at a period when historical landscape still ruled in all its rigour. As in literature

nothing was talked but the Noble style. There were no such
things as rivers, they were *torrents ;* no houses, but *Greek
temples ;* no peasants, but *shepherds* and *nymphs ;* no familiar
trees even, no simple elms nor commonplace birches, but *cedars*
and *palms* 'à la bonne heure !'"

Hence Corot's attachment to classical subjects, which Courbet
is reported to have jeered at. "Corot?" he said. "Ah, yes,
Corot! The man who is for ever setting the same nymphs
dancing in the same landscape." "Yes!" replies Silvestre,
"but how differently from his teachers he understood that
mythology! What youthfulness he brought into it! Is there
any other example of such complete originality applied to such
superannuated themes?"

It was not till the year 1825 that Corot became free of the
school of Bertin and went to Rome, when his first essay at
independent work gave him disheartening evidence of the waste
he had incurred of his student years. "I had spent two
winters with M. Bertin," he wrote to M. Silvestre, "learning
so little that on my arrival at Rome I could not draw in the
least. Two men stopped to chat together. I began to sketch
them, a part at a time—the head, for instance. They sepa-
rated, and I had nothing but some bits of head on my paper.
Some children were sitting on the steps of a church. I began
again. Their mother called them away, and my book would
be full of ends of noses, foreheads, and tresses of hair. I determined that I would not come home another time without a
piece of work *d'ensemble ;* and I tried for the first time a drawing *par masse,* a rapid drawing, the only kind possible. I set
myself, then, to outline, in the wink of an eye, the first
group I found ; if it only stayed a short time, I had, at any
rate, caught the character, the general *désinvolture ;* if it stayed

long enough, I could get at the details. I made a number of these exercises, and I have even succeeded in catching, in a few lines on a scrap of paper at the bottom of my hat, the ballets and scenic decorations of the opera."

"And that," says M. J. Rousseau, "was the mission of Corot; to catch nature alive, on the wing, in the midst of the eternal movement of things; and, for that purpose, to limit himself to *decisive accents:* to insist upon them ; to sacrifice the rest. Is not that—will not that be henceforth—the whole of his æsthetics?"

M. Dumesnil gleaned from Corot's conversation some details of the life of the community of painters at Rome. It was in the years 1825 to 1827 that Corot was there on his first visit. There were there, of young French painters, at that time, Léopold Robert, Schnetz, Aligny, Édward Bertin (of the *Journal des Débats*), Bodinier, and others. Chenavard arrived in 1827, when Corot was about returning home. They formed a French Academy there under the direction of Pierre Guérin.

It was to Aligny that Corot attributed the success of his whole career. In the Restaurant *della Lepre*, or at the *Café Grec*, their places of assembling, Corot made himself welcome as a good companion, singing—

" Je sais attacher les rubans,
Je sais comment poussent les roses,"

which M. Dumesnil tells us was a *Romance à la mode;* but his companions took no kind of notice of his work as a painter, only Aligny was occasionally sarcastic on the subject, until one day he found him working upon his study of the *Coliseum*, detected extraordinary merit in the work, and told his companions that "nobody had done that since Claude Lorrain."

The little picture was tardily exhibited afterwards in the Salon of 1849, and was a great success.*

It is characteristic of Corot that he never forgot nor depreciated what Aligny had then done for him :—his respect, his veneration never failed, and years after, when he was an eminent man himself, M. Hanoteau, whom he took to Aligny's studio one day (in the rue Monsieu. le Prince) says that Corot's behaviour to Aligny was "that of a timid shy boy before his master." Aligny, who died at Lyons in 1871, after the war, was buried in 1874 at Mont Parnasse, and at eight in the winter morning Corot was there.

"It was scarcely daylight, and the snow was falling and melting as it touched the earth; the sky was as wan and gloomy as the scene it overhung; there were but few persons there, and all the surroundings added to the sadness of the ceremony. Madame Aligny, seeing that Corot was shivering with cold, came and begged him to go away, but he would not. In the afternoon of the same day, he told me these details. A ray of sunshine was piercing the mist. 'Ah!' he said, 'it is better weather now than this morning in the cemetery; but it was a *devoir* to me—a sacred debt to pay.' Could he better express," says M. Dumesnil, "more delicately, or more simply, that the lapse of half a century left his memory faithful to the old act of kindness in Cæsar's gardens at Rome ?'"

The drawings of this period (of his first stay in Rome), says Dumesnil, may be easily recognised, for firmness and precision, for being very precise in execution, and nothing in them left to the imagination, as we shall find in his later works; and, as

* A wood engraving of it is to be seen in the "Histoire des Artistes Vivants" of Theo. Silvestre, *édition infolio.*

a special mark of them, they contain ink lines to better define the outlines.   He went to Naples and made some studies

THE RUIN, BY COROT.

In the possession of Hamilton Bruce, Esq.

there.   It is uncertain whether he visited Venice, but it has been suggested that the *View of the Grand Canal* is of this date. "It was, more likely, done in 1835," says Dumesnil. It is from M. Alfred Robaut, writing of the *chefs-d'œuvre* at the posthumous sale of his works in 1875, that I have gleaned the curious information that three of his Roman pictures, *The Coliseum*, *The Forum*, and a third picture (No. 17 of the posthumous sale) were all painted in the month of March, 1826. They were painted altogether in eighteen sittings, one picture in the morning, another about noon, and the third in the evening of the same days.

II.

Corot returned to France in 1827, and made his début in the Salon of the same year, with the *View taken at Narni* and the *Campagna of Rome*; and was hung between the two English painters, Bonington and Constable ; and, from this date until the year 1875, he never—with one exception—failed to take his part in the "Bataille des Expositions"; and in that year, in which he died, he left behind him three pictures for exhibition in the forthcoming Salon. He found in the annual contest the only jarring element in his otherwise almost ideally perfect life, and year by year stubbornly presented his work to the judgment of detractors, friends, and the unprejudiced public, until he had wrested from the critics and the juries praise which was their own blame ; and yet what a continual trial these Salons must have been to him ! The critics of the day passed his work unnoticed, all his pictures came back to him unsold, the public suspected some hoax underlying the antithesis to all that they had been accustomed to, and his

work was always badly hung. As M. Desbarrolles writes, in the
Bulletin de l'Ami des Arts of 1844 :—

"The artists say to the public, 'This man belongs to us—
you cannot comprehend him,' and the public begin to analyse
his work like a Chinese puzzle, and answer, 'It is possible.
No! I do not comprehend'; and so the simplest man in the
world passes for a man full of mannerism.

"Then he is never seen—he is always put out of sight, in
the dark galleries that they call the Catacombs. We will prove
this. Where was his *Hagar* put ?—In the Catacombs. His
View of the Tyrol ?—Catacombs. His *Little Apple Gatherers ?*—
Catacombs. His *Nymphs at the Bath ?*—Catacombs. His
Flute Player ?—Catacombs. But this last had such a success
that they took it out of the Catacombs, and hung it opposite a
window, in a blaze of light—a situation which they thought
bad enough for his *Democritus* the following year. . . . .
I remember, eight years ago, M. Corot had exhibited a picture
of white foreground, with the sea and a convent in the
distance ; it was of a ravishing harmony. Of course it was
hung in the Catacombs. We thrust a pen in his hand, and
forced him against his will to remonstrate. Did they change
it ? *Parbleu !* They hung it opposite, close to a blazing
window, and if you wanted to look at it, you had to put your
hat over the window in order to see the picture."

But the Salon, his battle-field, the *amari aliquid* of his cup of
life, was no tragedy, and the compensations that he enjoyed
were most enviable. The minute, affectionate particularity of
the biographical notices of him from which we draw our own,
shows the kind of attachment that he inspired and reciprocated
among his friends ; and in the critical world, he found himself
at an early period the centre of a group of partisans and

THE ENTRANCE TO A VILLAGE. BY COROT. *From the Collection of M. Detrimont.*

admirers none the less zealous, certainly, for their position in
face of the academical enemy. He was not left to fight alone.
Moreover, he was independent of his market; his allowance
was small, but his habits were simple. As his friend Albert
Wolff says : " Round about him others were struggling, from
day to day, for their daily bread, and to the rebellious thoughts that
groaned at the bottom of their hearts, they gave expression in
those terrible pictures, in which all things crumble to dust
beneath the storm—which were like a pictorial reflection of
their own tormented lives." But Corot knew nothing of this
gloom. " He enjoys laughing, he tells stories with animation,
he perpetrates practical jokes. And this jolly fellow is the
painter, so pure, of so many masterpieces of art ! the Orpheus
who has revived the ring of the Dryads under the foliage
of the sacred woods ! The magician who locks up a world
within a landscape vague, powdery, silvery, bathed in a light
divine !

" Once again, look at him well ! Under that gaiety, melancholy lurks ; and that laugh does not silence the voice of the
soul. Corot is a poet of emotion (*ému*), who gives his good
humour free play at his own times and seasons. Above all, he
is a true artist and lover of his art, living far from all noise, in
face of a beloved canvas, making of the studio a cell, and of
every place a studio, dreaming and seeking, above all *finding*—
good, amiable, beloved, and," adds M. Jules Clarétie, " (it is no
mean praise) full of respect for his art."

M. Clarétie might have found a nobler name than melancholy for the peaceful side of his picture. Corot, throughout
his life and to the end of it, was subject to a master sentiment
of gratitude for the immunities, and the lofty enjoyments that
had fallen to his lot. He was no ordinary character, and the
zest with which his personal friends dwell upon his passing

words and doings is amply justified by the beauty and the healthful nature of the subject; "and his genius," says Wolff, "was as cheerful as his disposition; his personal character—the tender feeling that he has for all that touches his heart—finds its reflection in his works—the '*note souriante*' of the whole man, happy in the mere enjoyment of living and breathing the scented air of the fields which seems to float about his landscapes and to 'invade' the student of his pictures"; and almost the last words of his life, recorded by Français, to whom they were spoken a few hours only before his death, resume our subject and justify the affection that he inspired:—"Truly," he said, "if my hour has come I shall have nothing to complain of. For fifty-three years I have been a painter. I have, therefore, been permitted to devote myself entirely to that which I loved the most in the world. I have never suffered from poverty; I have had good parents and excellent friends. I can only be thankful to GOD."

When in Paris, Corot occupied a small apartment in the Faubourg Poissonnière, and a modest painting-room on the fourth floor. He shared also with his sister a cottage at Ville-d'Avray, where he retired to nature and was undisturbed. There are many descriptions of him; Jules Clarétie gives an illustration of an incident in his Paris life :—

"In a little theatre the other evening they were playing a vaudeville, when I saw a man enter whom I recognised at once. Carelessly dressed in a fashion of the past he seemed out of place. . . . . His fatherly face, his complexion coloured and embrowned by work in the open air, his iron-grey hair, 'brushed by a squall of wind,' give him a likeness to some peaceable farmer. But look at his face! How it suddenly wakens to life and lights up! The illumination replaces the *illuminure;* the man from the country disappears, the artist is here. The head is powerful and large, and yet the features are fine; the nose is straight, outlined in one *trait;* the mouth, which seems fond of smiling, is habitually partly open, like that of one who is lost in thought; but, above all, look at that forehead! That pure brow, surmounted by the fine hair, well planted, tangled, floating free! It seems to be a depository of a whole world of dreams. The eye *va et vient,* brilliant, *spirituel,* then suddenly stops and assumes a singular fixity. All this physiognomy is made of two elements, gaiety and thought—the lips smile, the look meditates."

The incident which M. Clarétie goes on to narrate is the entrance into an opposite box of the theatre of a beautiful lady, and M. Corot, in the depths of his hat, working at a sketch of her, furtively glancing from side to side to see whether he is doing so unnoticed.

But of his own life in the country Corot has bequeathed in a very long letter to a friend a description which is an auto-biography in itself. The absolute necessity of condensing it at all is a calamity—the letter should be seen at length; it is an idyll of the most perfect poetry. The quaint introduction of ejaculations imitating musical effects is characteristic.* The letter is addressed to Mr. Stevens Graham, and is reproduced by Jules Clarétie, and almost all other biographers of .Corot:—

"A landscape painter's day is delightful. He gets up early, at three in the morning, before sunrise. He goes and sits under a tree, and watches, and waits.

"There is not much to be seen at first.

"Nature is behind a white veil, on which some masses of

* Corot was passionately fond of music; Wolff calls him "the Mozart of Painting." ·

C

form are vaguely indicated. Everything smells sweet. Everything trembles under the invigorating breezes of the dawn.

"*Bing!* The sun is becoming clear, and begins to rend the veil of gauze behind which the meadow, and the valley, and the hills on the horizon hide. The vapours of night still hang, like silver tufts, on the cold green grass.

"*Bing! Bing!* The sun's first ray— Another ray— The little flowers seem to be waking in a joyful mood, and each one of them is drinking its drop of quivering dew. The leaves feel the cold, and are moving to and fro in the morning air. Under the leaves the unseen birds are singing—*it sounds as if the flowers were saying their morning prayer.* Amoretti with butterfly wings are perching on the meadow, and set the tall grasses swaying.

" 'On n'y voit rien ; tout y est !' We can see *nothing*—but the landscape is *there*, all perfect behind the translucent gauze of the mist which rises—rises—rises, inhaled by the sun ; and, as it rises, discloses the river silver-scaled, the meads, the trees, the cottages, the vanishing distance. We can distinguish now all that we divined before. (*Now the note changes.*) "*Bam!* the sun is risen. *Bam!* a peasant crosses the field, and a cart and oxen. *Ding, Ding!* says the bell of the ram who leads the flock of sheep. *Bam!* All things break forth into glistening, and glittering, and shining in a full flood of light, of pale caressing light, as yet. . . . . It is adorable! and I paint—and I paint!

"Oh, the beautiful red cow plunged in the wet grass to her dewlap! I will paint her. Here is Simon looking over my shoulder.

" 'Well, Simon, what do you think of that ?'

" 'Oh, dame ! m'sieu ; it's beautiful.'

" 'And you see what it's meant for, eh ?'

" 'I should think so ! It's a big yellow rock !'

"*Boum! Boum!* The sun grows hot—the flowers droop—the birds are silent. Let us go home! We can see *too much* now. There is nothing in it.

"And home we go, and dine, and sleep, and dream; and I dream of the morning landscape. I dream my picture, and presently I will paint my dream."

(*The Nocturne is equally delightful.*) "*Bam, Bam!*" he cries, "the sun is setting now, in an *explosion* of yellow, of orange, of rouge-feu,* of cherry, of purple. Ah! that is pretentious and vulgar—I don't like that; I shall wait, and so will the patient, thirsty flowers, who know that the Sylphs of evening are presently coming to sprinkle them with vapours of dews from their invisible *arrosoirs;* and, at last, with a final *Boum!* of purple and gold the sun sinks out of sight. Good Lord! how beautiful it is! The sun has disappeared, and in the softened sky has only left behind a gauzy, vapourous tint of the palest lemon, which melts and blends into the deep dark blue of the Night, through all the tones of deepening green, of pallid turquoise, of inconceivable fineness, of a delicacy fluid and inappreciable."

As night draws on, and he watches "the dark water reflecting the sweet tones of the sky," mystery returns: "We can see it no more, we feel that it is all still there." Then Nature falls asleep, "while still the fresh evening breeze is sobbing through the foliage, and the birds—those voices of the flowers—are singing Evening Prayer." . . . .

"*Bing!* a star in the sky pricks its portrait in the pond"—anon a second star—"three—six—twenty stars! All the stars in the sky have made a tryst to meet in this fortunate pond! All around now is darkness and gloom—only the little lake is sparkling—an ant-heap of busy stars." . . . . (*Finally.*) "The

* Rouge-feu comes in the scale between r. *incarnat*, and r. *safrané*, which passes on through r. *orange* and r. *chair* to *rose.—Littré.*

sun has gone to rest.   The inner Sun—the Sun of the soul—
the sun of Art is rising.   Good! my picture is made!"

AN EVENING IN NORMANDY.   BY COROT.

In the possession of Hamilton Bruce Esq.

The sentiment of Corot's poetry is relieved by a fine vein of
humour—as in a page which we have omitted of the letter
quoted above, he talks of "the little round weeping willows

turning somersaults along the bank of the river." He was full
of similar fancies, and absolutely childish about the figures that
he introduced into his landscapes, because "he could not live
there all alone." "Look at that shepherdess leaning against
the tree," he said. "There! she is startled now, she heard a
rat running about in the grass." "When I come home from
an excursion," he told Silvestre, "I invite Nature to come and
pass a few days in my house. Then my madness sets in.
With my brush in my hand I go out nutting through the
woods, in my studio; and, still there, I can hear the birds
singing, and the trees rustling in the wind; and I can see the
streams and the rivers flowing on, carrying thousands of mirror
pictures of the sky and the land; and the sun rises and sets in
my own house for me!"

In his life he knew the "happiness of having no history."
Its incidents are few and not remarkable. Soon after the
Salon of 1833, he returned to Italy—to the north of Italy this
time; and did not go on to Rome, but to Venice. He returned
without completing his contemplated tour, in obedience to a
letter from his father expressing anxiety at his long absence.
The anxiety of the father, and the docility of the son, are
characteristic, for Camille was a boy of thirty-seven years of
age at the time. Amongst other work, he brought home with
him some marine studies, and views taken in the Italian Tyrol;
also the *motif* for a landscape with figures, called *Diana
Surprised at the Bath*, which was exhibited in the following
year along with that *Campagna of Rome* noticed by Alfred de
Musset in the *Revue des Deux Mondes*. Noticed!—to this
extent—"Corot, whose *Campagna de Rome* finds admirers."
That was all, but Corot, to whom, at the age of forty, this was
the first, *very small* taste of success, was elated and grateful

that his name should even have been written by so great
a poet—and painted a picture at once on the subject of De
Musset's stanzas to the Evening Star.*

Silvestre thinks the Italian climate "*fortified* Corot's talent,"
which naturally tended to an excess in softness and indecision.

In 1843, Corot made a third voyage to Italy, remaining
there about half a year, during which, at Genoa, he painted a
Vue générale of that city remarkable for the clear and *limpid*
light pervading it.   In Italy, also, he brought to perfection his
study of the " values of tones," so that, as Silvestre expresses
it, " he could arrange judiciously the scheme of a landscape,
precisely as if he were putting together the fragments of a
mosaic," and so he painted all his views of Italian scenery :
*Volterra ; The Volcanic Lands near Marino ; Florence, from the
Garden of the Grand Duke ; Rome, from the Campo Vaccino, the
Coliseum*, &c.   But twenty years later, the same critic writes :
"I like better his poplars fine and light as feathers, his skies of
Ville-d'Avray, grey and soft, his green meads of Normandy,
his quiet river banks of Villeneuve-Saint-Georges than the rocks
of Subiaco, or the ravines of Volterra, or the rent crags of
Marino."   " Je me suis laissé encotonner par le ciel cotonneux
de Paris," said Corot himself (untranslatably).

In 1847, Corot was decorated with the Legion of Honour,
and his family began to understand him, and his father began
to say : "I think I might allow Camille a little more money."
And, in the meantime, Camille had become a grey-headed man !

* " Pâle étoile du soir, messagère lointaine,
   Dont le front sort brillant des voiles du couchant,
   De ton palais d'azur, au sein du firmament,
    Que regardes-tu dans la plaine ? "

[It is very like Leopardi's " *Che fai tu, luna, in cielo ?* "]

From a photograph by M. Georges Petit.]

THE REED CUTTER. BY COROT.

But still, for the space of another lifetime, for a quarter of a century more, he has to struggle on, for ever fighting with the persistent opposition of those in authority, to whom the doctrines in Art that he exemplified were as poison. We have alluded already to this side of our subject. Our space is too small to recapitulate. We pass on to the closing scenes of his long, laborious, and tranquil life of *pax in bello*. More space than is allotted to us for his whole biography could be occupied by an account of his acts of beneficence, and his sympathy, and his gratuitous teaching of young painters, and his giving away of his work here and there, and the sincerity of his creed that what he gave to the poor he *lent* to a Divine Benefactor, and how, when he was remonstrated with on the subject, he allowed, " Yes ! a thousand francs was a *pull*, but only the next day I sold six thousand francs' worth of my paintings. *It all comes back again*." And how, in 1870, when he saw that the siege of Paris was inevitable, he returned thither, and remained there all the time ; and in ambulances, and in relief of the famished poor, he spent himself and his substance,* working hard all the time at his art, without which, he said, " I should have gone crazy."

When he was told of the death of Millet, he was a dying man himself, and it was from his own deathbed that he took instant measures for the comfort of the widow and her nine children, of the friend whom he was to follow, in five-weeks' time, to that " world that sets this world right."

We must pass over also the hundreds of genial, gossiping anec dotes told so carefully by his intimate friends, which make the study of his biography, entirely apart from its art interest such interesting reading, and above all, we must leave to other hands the appreciation, year by year, of the lesson that he was

---

* It is said that he gave away more than 25,000 francs (£1,000).

silently teaching painters, the justification of his instinct of exhibition, that none of the lessons that Nature taught him (through the sympathies of his own nature so much more than by any technic endowment of hand and eye) should be lost to the world.

His contribution to the Salon of 1874 resumed a great deal of his work. Dumesnil calls it, using a musical figure, "A Symphony of the Hours of Day," the brilliance of light, the half-tint of twilight, the shadow of night. The pictures were named *Souvenir d'Arleux*, *Le Soir*, *Le Clair de Lune*.

In October of this year, his sister, with whom, since their father's death, he had shared the cottage at Ville-d'Avray, died; and her death fell upon him, his friends say, "like a summons." From the day that it happened his own hitherto fine health declined rapidly. He was already very ill in December of that year, when a grand fête was given in his honour at the Grand Hôtel, for the presentation of the gold medal that the artists had prepared for him.

The medal was presented, his health was drunk with ringing and prolonged acclamations, and Corot whispered to M. Marcotte, who presided, "It is a very happy thing for a man to feel himself beloved like this!" "Alas!" says Dumesnil, "how changed he was! His furrowed features told their tale of suffering; the face of former days was gone; nervous and feverish, he made efforts which exceeded his powers, spoke with animation, and would remain standing."

He lingered for about two months after this final scene of triumph and of "Farewell!" He went to his studio at times, but he could not work, but liked to sit there among his memories of the past.

"And often," says Dumesnil, "my memory carries me thither still, to sit by the side of the Master in his work-

IN THE MARSHES. BY COROT.
In the Collection of P. H. Sears, Esq., ''

man's blouse, and smoking cap, chatting on all subjects while his powerful hand, adapted for the heaviest labour, held the light brush producing his charming works."

He had finished his pictures for the Salon of 1875, *Biblis* and *The Pleasures of Evening*, when he ceased to work in his studio. They only wanted signing, and were brought to him in his bed, when he could no longer rise, and he signed them there, and fell back and said, "Behold all that I can do !" It was the last time that he touched his brush. In the partial delirium of his last moments, what thoughts were left him were still occupied with his art ; " he moved his right hand to the wall, his fingers seemed to be holding a brush, and he said to his friend, ' Look ! how beautiful ! I have never seen such admirable landscapes !' and with these words he died, on Tuesday, the 23rd of February, 1875."

We have taken the above details from the narrative of M. Dumesnil, who closes them appropriately with the following quotation :—

> " Terre, soleil, vallons, belle et douce nature,
> Je vous dois une larme au bord de mon tombeau ;
> L'air est si parfumé ! La lumière est si pure !
> Aux regards d'un mourant le soleil est si beau ! "
> [*Lamartine, Méditations Poétiques*, xxv.]

III.

The writers who have supplied us with the details of Corot's biography seem all to be contending which of them was capable of loving the old man most; I have never studied such a literature before—the work of a number of men, eminent in letters themselves, individually differing in character, not forming a côterie; but the only link of their separate writings, the sort of gospel

of good-nature in the midst of fierce disputes, which Corot
seems to have carried about in his genial open hand.

Corot was not strikingly epigrammatic himself; the poetry
in him was rather subtle and diffused; but he was the cause
of much epigram in others, and this is a proof of his hold upon
their minds, for the epigram is, or should be, the expression of
long digested thought. "Corot," says Ernest Chesneau, "dwells
in a planet of his own, and rules a kingdom that is serious and
charming, but he is a sovereign who has no subjects."

On the same point M. Gustave Planche wrote, in early times
(1838): " Whilst there are whole caravans of painters dividing
France among them, and copying a copse, a bush, a hedge, or
a stream, and counting the stones by the side of a ditch, it is a
good thing to have earnest men, like M. Corot, who disdain
such vulgar reality, and set themselves to introduce *invention*
into landscape. Whether he will succeed or not, we cannot
say, but we hope the crowd will give him the credit due
to his efforts; for the landscapes of M. Corot are a useful
protest against the finicking realism that threatens to invade
our school. He has a care for the ideal, and his ambition
deserves applause."

A hostile critic of the classical school, M. Lenormant, in
very early days (1833), wrote: "M. Corot takes his inspiration from Fontainebleau, but if he had not been to Italy,
he would not have seen the forest of Fontainebleau as
he has seen, and rendered it." The same critic admitted,
on another occasion, that Corot's painting of water was
"more transparent than Ruysdael." But M. Charles Timbal,
apostrophising Fromentin, growls: "What is all this foliage
with no leaves? Leave this slovenly work to its own inventors!
When you have the power of being Fromentin, what caprice,
or what motive, pushes you to try to be Corot?"

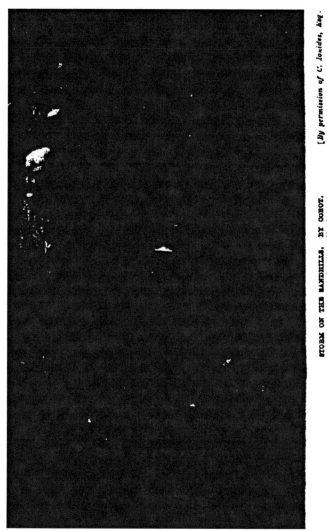

STORM ON THE SANDHILLS. BY COROT.
Formerly in the Ionides Collection.

[*By permission of C. Ionides, Esq.*

"Truly," says a writer in the *Bulletin de l'Ami des Arts* (1844), "the charm of a picture is the affection that the artist expends upon it, and with Corot, love—incessant longing for that which rejoices and satisfies the heart—spreads over every part of his composition." "Corot is a unique painter," writes M. Edmond About; "outside of all styles, and of all schools; he is no imitator; he imitates nothing, *not even Nature;* and he is inimitable. . . . . He transmutes all that he touches; he appropriates all that he paints; he never copies, and even when he is working from Nature, he is inventing—not copying; he could not copy one of his own pictures!"

Another interesting paper in the same magazine in the same year discusses the advantage, or disadvantage, of study in Rome. After selecting Jolivard, Dupré, and Rousseau, for the home representatives; and Cabat, Corot, and Marilhat, for the Roman trained, the writer enters upon a valuation of the merit of each; calls Jolivard, "the French Hobbema"; Jules Dupré, "an artist full of force and light, who seems to make new progress every year," and saying that "one of Rousseau's pictures of the present time would lose nothing in the museum by companionship with the ancient masters—the day will come that will prove it!"—goes on to complain of the travellers, Cabat and Marilhat, rendering justice to their power, but objecting to their "embellishment of nature." "Cabat, especially," he says, "is getting to be altogether too 'ideal,' painting nothing but that which he considers *noble*." "But Corot is an original artist, in a road that belongs only to himself. He yields to his own two impulses—of Poetry, and of Truth. His pictures always shine with naïve grace, with true observation of Nature, delicious harmony, and a poetical sentiment. We recognise in the nobility of his lines and composition, the talent of a man trained in a country favoured by the sky."

The subject of the influence of Italy was always a vexed question. An amusing little novel, in the *Revue de Paris*, has for its chief hero : "Blaise, a young painter, who reckoned in the catalogue of his 'belles qualités' that of never having been to Rome"; and he makes the most life-like pictures of cabbages in a back garden, *because he has seen them*, and boasts that he is not one of those who "desire to lead people back to religion by means of Art, or to convert them·to Christianity with Prussian blue." Blaise did not want to convert anybody to anything; he painted cabbages. This falls in with a phrase I have noted from Dumesnil's work on Corot : "There are limits to the admiration due to skill, and it is impossible to get up a poetical sentiment over a bunch of turnips."

There is a very large fund of anecdote about Corot to draw from in the reminiscences of his friends. Dumesnil tells this :— In 1851 Corot was vexed that nobody paused to look at his landscape, which was, as usual, badly hung in the Salon, and the fancy struck him that he would stand before it and look at it himself. "People are like flies," he thought, "as soon as one comes to a dish the others congregate; if I stand here I shall attract the passers-by." A young couple presently approached the picture, and Corot waited impatiently to hear what they would say. The bridegroom's remark was favourable. "That is not bad. I think there is something *in* that." But his wife, "the softest and gentlest little person!" Corot used to say, drew her husband away from the picture, saying, "It is frightful! *Allons nous en!*" and I, said Corot, said to myself, "Art thou satisfied ? Thou hast heard the opinion of the public!"

Corot, as his pictures suggest, was passionately fond of music, and seldom let slip an opportunity of listening to the best performances. He went to the theatre a great deal, and, M. Dumesnil observes, " in his later years could see traces of his own influence in some of the scenery." He had an excellent voice for singing, and knew by heart a great deal of modern music, and sang the great Italian airs with spirit and taste. He himself compared his pictures to " little songs." M. Silvestre relates of him that he was standing one day before a great picture of Delacroix, and said, " He is an eagle. I am only a skylark. *Je pousse de petites chansons dans mes nuages gris.*" " When I find myself in the fields," he said once, " I fly into a rage with my pictures."

He was not fond of reading. He read the same book over and over again, and an extremely ponderous work he selected. It was Corneille's Polyeuctes, Martyr : tragédie Chrétienne—in 5 Acts (*published at Naples*, 1773). " For twenty years he has been going over the first two hundred verses of this tragedy, but never gets to the end of it, and when he talks of reading he says, 'But this year I must finish Polyeuctes!'"

In his dealing with his pupils Corot was free from pedantry, and advised them in the choice of subjects to be guided by the sympathy of their own *impressions*, judging, as M. Silvestre expresses it, " that the soul of each artist is a mirror in which Nature comes to reflect herself in a peculiar manner."

The sentiment might be more clearly expressed. It is the foundation of what was called the " Impressionist" school of landscape—" paysage intime "—" *Stimmungslandschaft,*" a German critic calls it, " wherein the subjective impression is expressed in a " *Naturbild,*" and the painter's object is to hold fast, maintain the *Stimmung* throughout the whole of his picture."

He never would receive payment for his lessons. Français

THE DANCE OF THE NYMPHS. BY COROT. *In the Louvre.*

was his favourite pupil, whose natural style, even before his tuition had an affinity to that of Corot. He was twenty years of age when he was introduced to Corot by Buttura. The beautiful lithograph reproductions that he made of Corot's work are well known. Corot had a deaf and dumb boy for one of his pupils, and for a first lesson he wrote down the word "CONSCIENCE," and underlined it with three strokes. The pupil, like the Chinese tailor in the old story who reproduced the patch in the new clothes, copied a drawing so scrupulously that he did not omit a blot of glue that had fallen upon it, and Corot laughed and told him, "If you look at Nature as carefully as that you will find her faultless, no spot upon *her !*" Daubigny was another pupil who owed much to Corot. "Another landscape painter, one of the first of our time, whose beginnings were rough, was always supported and guided by Corot. M. Daubigny well knows how, in hours of depression, his master appeared, as if by chance, and just in time to wind him up with good advice and praises."

Finally, a short notice is due to Corot's work in the grand style, directed to religious subjects. It is little known, but considered by some writers to be of high importance. In 1835 he painted a *Hagar in the Wilderness,* and in the following year a *S. Jérôme,* which he presented in 1849 to the church at Ville-d'Avray, and in 1840 he exhibited in the Salon a *Flight into Egypt,* and a *Monk,* and in 1841 a *Democritus,* and all these paintings M. Silvestre looks upon as a sort of prelude to his grand religious composition of the *Baptism of Christ,* which he painted on his return from Rome, in 1843, for the Bapistery chapel of the church of S. Nicholas du Chardonnet.

"There can be no doubt of his having done that painting

after his second or third voyage in Italy. The magnificent landscape (on the left as you enter the chapel) in which the Baptism of Christ is represented, quite recalls in character and style the first drawings that he did when he was with Aligny in the *agro romano,* under the clear Italian sky. The whole is a large panel, well fitted with trees of a delicate foliage, a river, and in the far off perspective, monuments of a proud city. But the most extraordinary feature of this work is the *figures,* of which there are nine, besides the angel hovering in the sky; they are all of the size of life, well grouped, in fine attitudes, and done so that a painter of History might sign them. This painting is a revelation of his power and aptitude for the "Grand Art," as Titian, Poussin, and the real Great Masters, including Rembrandt, understood it.

MONUMENT TO COROT.   BUST BY JEOFFROY DE CHAUNE.
Erected by the painter's friends at Ville d' Avray.

D

PORTRAIT OF DAUBIGNY. BY HIMSELF.

CHARLES FRANÇOIS DAUBIGNY.

C HARLES FRANÇOIS DAUBIGNY was born on the
15th of February, 1817, at Paris, in the Rue des Rosiers,
au Marais, in a household much occupied with Art, and took
up his apprenticeship to the profession, systematically, in his
childhood, when his playthings were pencils and paints, and
began his career of useful and beautiful production as a boy
under the guidance of friends familiar with the channels of
employment in the humbler industrial artist ranks. Literally
from his nursery to his grave he was a man who sufficed for
himself and those dependent on his aid by art work. Like
Rembrandt or Meissonier, the source of his genius was the
power—the love—of incessant, unremitted *work*. He combined
with this passion of industry a characteristic that is its common
companion, an extraordinary geniality and light-heartedness,
and with this a love of outdoor activity and athletic amuse-
ment, especially boating; and he was loud and hearty in his
speech and boisterous in manner, and his friends nicknamed
him Captain Daubigny.*

His father, Edmé-François Daubigny, was a poor man, a
drawing-master, a pupil himself of Victor Bertin. He painted

* "Par son intelligence vive et alerte, par sa mobilité d'esprit et son
insouciante gaieté, il resta toujours un enfant de Paris."—*Henriet.*

for exhibition little domestic pictures of scenery and semi-
rustic life about the suburbs of Paris, and taught his son, at a
very early age, to do the same. He was born in the terrible
year 1789. He appears to have had the good fortune to live
quietly, and escape conscription, through the Napoleonic era,
and made his *début* in the Salon of 1819.*

There were also of the family an uncle, Pierre Daubigny,†
and an aunt, Amélie, the wife of Pierre, who were both
miniature painters, pupils of d'Aubry, and regular exhibitors
in the Salons, where the aunt won medals. She had a sister,
Henriette-Virginie Dautel, who had also some success as a
painter of miniatures.

The mother of Daubigny, whose maiden name was Legros-
d'Anizy, died when he was twelve years of age. He was a
weak and sickly child, and was sent to the country for some
years to an old nurse who lived at Valmondois, near the Isle-
Adam. ‡ M. Henriet (to whom we are indebted for the details
of his biography) says: "It is among the apple orchards, in
the pure air of the open country, that he passed his earlier
years, and imbibed that love of the fields which became the
passion of his life. Whenever, in later days, he can escape

* He exhibited landscapes from the suburbs of Paris in the Salons of
1819, 1822, 1831, 1833, 1842, &c. About 1835 he was taken to Italy, as a
Professor, in the family of the Marquis de la Grange (this would be in his
son's eighteenth year), and subsequently exhibited views of Italy in the
Salons of 1837, 1838, 1839, and 1841. He died at Paris in 1843.

† PIERRE DAUBIGNY (1795—1858) exhibited miniatures at all the Salons
from 1822 to 1855. It must have been he who left the legacy to his
nephew in 1858.

‡ Isle-Adam is a romantic part of the Oise, where the windings of the
river form three small islands; on the largest there was built the castle of
Adam, the Constable, in the reign of Philippe I., A.D. 1019. The Forest
of Isle-Adam contains about 4,000 acres, is about nine miles in length,
and is celebrated for magnificent oaks.

from the great Parisian hive, and steal from his daily labour a clear day in the sunshine, he will run to Valmondois, to the cottage and orchard of his childhood, to the kind 'old nurse' who receives him open-armed. This is the origin of his love for the banks of the Oise, which determined him, when he became rich, to build his country residence at Auvers."

There is an interesting picture of this playground of his childhood in an illustration that he made to a story, in "l'Artiste," in 1842, representing a Normandy wedding procession passing, on a sunny day, through corn-fields, which are a clearing snugly embosomed in a wood; and, peeping out of the apple-trees on the right-hand corner, is the picturesque thatched cottage of Madame Bazot—for all the world a scene in Devonshire. The child whose playthings were pencil and paint no doubt had made ruder sketches of this pastoral solitude. Rustic solitudes must have been through life to him always like memories of his childhood, and his feeling for the moods of landscape is misnamed in calling it romantic, unless we apply the term to a child's imaginative creations, for all the multitude of Daubigny's paintings, etchings, and book illustrations are alike—an impulsive, naïve simplicity characterizes them all, town scenes and country scenes alike; and it is only when he forces himself into classical, unreal spheres that he fails signally to command either sympathy or admiration (his *St. Jerome* of 1840, for example).

We are told that, his father marrying again, he left home at an early age, and maintained himself independently by the proceeds of his own work. He had begun to earn money before this, contributing to the insufficient resources of the household in a variety of employments—painting snuff-boxes, panel decorations, picture clocks, and similar objects. He was filling his portfolios also with sketches made in the streets, along the quays on the banks of the Seine, in the Boulevard du Temple, in the city markets, in the Zoological Gardens, and elsewhere ; and his engraved work, from these and similar sketches, in the books that he illustrated a few years later on, harmonizes admirably with that of his colleagues in the same books, especially Meissonier's, with the distinction that the latter worked directly upon the human interest of a scene, and Daubigny upon the accessories, which he reduced instinctively to a pleasant harmony, indicating, above all, the presence and the *movement* of *air*. The touch of genius, or of taste, will be found in the slightest things that he produced among his earliest efforts —such as his pretty vignettes for trade circulars and invoices, pictures for advertising "houses to let," and similar trade illustrations. Amongst them is a fairy-like view of parks and gardens, and young girls in them disporting at skipping-rope and ball play, which he did for a suburban girls' school, kept by a Madame Dautel, a relative of his aunt Amélie. And among them also—a sign of the times—is a lithograph, after Fouyère, of the ideal *phalanstère*, or communistic settlement of Fourrier. In a few years we shall find Daubigny a member of a small phalanstère himself.* He must also have found leisure, in the midst of his work, to study at the same time painting and engraving, as he appears simultaneously in a few years as a professional engraver, a master in etching, and a landscape painter, exhibiting at the Salon and going near to winning the " blue ribbon " of that art—the landscape Prix de Rome. And he was not yet nineteen, and all the time he was putting by money !

M. Henriet makes quite a little romance of his narration

* A closer study of the contemporary development of this form of communism would repay the student of the biographies of these Barbizon painters and their champion Thoré.

The Flock of Geese. By Daubigny. *In the Millet Collection.*

how Daubigny, at this period of his youth, shared his lodgings and his money with his friend, Mignan, another art student, and how the two boys determined that they would go to Italy, and hoarded their small savings for that purpose day by day, not in a common cash-box, which they could open in a moment of weakness with a knife, but in a built-up hole in the wall of their room, which nobody could plunder without the help of a crowbar; and for a whole year the two friends worked hard and lived sparely, and kept no account, but lived in a delightful fever of uncertainty of the rate of accumulation of the deposit in the wall; and at the end of a year, in fear and trembling, they broke the wall open and let out a tinkling rivulet of small coins, which amounted to fourteen hundred francs; and with this wealth, and with gaiters and knapsacks, they bravely set out together and *walked to Italy*,* and visited Florence, and Rome, and Naples, sketching as they went, and finally settled down for four months at the old Roman watering-place of Subiaco, where, indeed, they might be excused for dreaming landscapes of the most classical antiquity.† And here Daubigny worked hard,

---

* "Daubigny and Mignan set out *sac au dos, guêtre au pied, le bâton à la main;* intoxicated with sunshine and liberty, they felt that all the world was their own. Their walk was one long enchantment, as they saw new perspectives open every moment before their eyes, and a succession of panoramas unrolled, at the richness, the *accent*, and the variety of which they marvelled. Beyond Lyons they recognised with ecstasy the presence of the South by the intenser light of the sky and the grandeur of the landscape, dressed in a vegetation unknown in our latitudes—the olive, the cypress, the plane-tree, the pine; all the beloved trees of the antique idyll. They passed at last across the delightful garden shut in on the left by the first mountains of the Alps, and on the right of them shone in the sunshine the peaks of the Cevennes. At last they trod the epic soil of Italy!"—*Henriet*.

† Subiaco is the old Roman *Sublacense cœnobium*, a place of great interest

as he always did, and doubtless did useful work, but Mignan
was distracted and impatient to get home again, being unfortu-
nately in love. And Daubigny, at the end of four months,
sympathised with this and agreed to return; and they *walked
home again*, and were met at Troyes, and escorted for the
remainder of the journey by a party of friends; and they
counted their money at Troyes, and found two louis d'ors of
it left, they having been away eleven months, their joint
expenditure being, therefore, five pounds a month. The love-
sick Mignan got married immediately, and left off painting,
and went into business; and Daubigny went, so to speak, into
business also, but still, in a manner, painted.

He obtained employment in the studio, or workshop, or
picture-hospital, of M. Granet, the keeper of the King's pictures,
which M. Granet is said to have been more zealous than
discreet in restoring. Critics say that in his years of office,
from 1826 to 1848, M. Granet did more mischief to the
national treasures than the treaties of 1815. Admirers of
Daubigny's 'prentice brush may look for traces of it on the
Titians and Leonardos in the Louvre. He became skilful "à
mastiquer les craquelures," but could not suppress his feeling
of horror at the acts of sacrilege that he assisted in; there
was an uproar on the subject in the studios, an official
investigation, and detection of his indiscretion, and he was
dismissed.

We place at this date a letter, of which a fac-simile is given

to the antiquarian as well as to the lover of nature. M. Henriet's volume
has a view of the town, from an etching by Daubigny—which has a weird
quality, like one of Doré's mediæval nightmares—a very tall-built, tower-
ing, old, closely-crowded city on a knoll overlooking a natural amphi-
theatre of rough, apparently volcano-blistered land, and in the foreground
massive-trunked old trees of impossible foliage, and a dark lake in the
background, and the whole scene itself shut in by loftier hills behind.

in "L'Art," dated from Dordrecht in Holland, 14th of September, 1836, or 1837 (the figures are scarcely legible), in which he writes: "Depuis 8 jours nous sommes dans la blonde Hollande, aussi blonde que les femmes de Rubens. Quel ravissant pays!" and goes on to say that he was on his way to the Hague and Amsterdam, and then home "at a gallop"; but "I could not come back without seeing Paul Potter's bull, and the 'Night Watch' of Rembrandt." . . . . . "We have hired a boat, and propose to work on the Meuse, where we *do* the mills of Dordrecht." His portfolio of sketches being produced to his friends, Henriet says, the best thing that he had brought home from Italy was a crayon drawing, finished with the utmost care, of a *thistle*; and Geoffroy Dechaume exclaimed: "Pardieu! *Thou* need not have gone to Rome for that; you would have found one at Montmartre!" In the letter quoted from Dordrecht, he sent an amusing scribbled sketch of himself under a large umbrella in a flat field, drawing a most matter-of-fact windmill, with a Dutch man and boy on each side of him pointing long fingers, one at the mill, the other at his easel, each wearing a long tapering nightcap, with tassels fluttering in the wind, indicating the direction of it like two weathercocks; and in the greater number of his out-of-door sketches, Daubigny's first care seems to have been to indicate the direction of the wind. We have now brought our narrative to the time when he was nineteen or twenty years of age (1836 or 1837), in the particular of self-help being already superior to most of his contemporaries, Millet, for example, who were much older men.

It is a noticeable thing that the men best fitted to run alone in life, are *not* those men who are fond of solitude in their independence, but of association. "Who shuns his friends, flies fortune in the concrete," they say. Daubigny had always a multitude of intimate friends, and with each and all of them some association in his work. Meissonier, for example, put in the figures to his etchings of *La Moine* and *La Tonnelle;* and so with others; but with three of his brother artists, Steinheil,* Geoffroy-Dechaume,† and Trimolet,‡ his connection was peculiar and domestic. It was Fourrierism again. These four formed themselves into a "phalanstère artistique," and lived together in a pleasant maisonnette, "planted in a kitchen garden" *(potager),* says M. Henriet, in the Rue des Amandières (Popincourt), and had all things in common; a common purse, a common table, common interests in life; worked on the same books together, and had a clause in their partnership that annually one should be enabled, at the expense of the others, to prepare a picture for exhibition in the Salon of the year. Daubigny had exhibited, in 1838, a view of the *Chevet* (Chancel end) of Notre Dame de Paris, and of the Île Saint Louis, at the end of the Île Louvois, which attracted no attention. They claimed the privilege in turns, but the turn of Daubigny came round again in 1840 (that is, the twenty-third of his age), and he sent in a *St. Jerome in the*

* Steinheil was principally employed in the illustration of books. He worked in an *ecclesiastical* style, and made drawings for the painters of glass of the saints in churches.

† Geoffroy-Dechaume was a sculptor and medallist, whose greatest honour was, perhaps, his selection by the Artists' Committee to design the medal of honour that they presented to Corot.

‡ Trimolet, illustrator of books, along with Tony Johannot, whom he was a close rival to, married Daubigny's sister. The story of his unfortunate failure in life is as sad as it is incomprehensible to any who have looked through the great multitude of books that he was employed upon. He seems to have possessed genius, industry, and all good and honourable personal qualities, but failed with all this to support himself, and the deaths of his wife first and of himself, almost simultaneously, were accelerated by sheer starvation. They left a boy, for whom Daubigny provided.

SHEPHERD AND SHEPHERDESS. FROM THE ETCHING BY DAUBIGNY.

Desert, which was hung by the side of a landscape of his father's, and may be dismissed with M. Henriet's description of it : "a terrible pile of rocks *à la Salvator*." *

In this year, 1840, on the 28th of July, was the Ceremony of Inauguration of the Column of July, on the Place de la Bastille. Trimollet and Daubigny speculated on this occasion in a picture of the ceremony, giving the Place de la Bastille as it then was, with great stacks of timber at the end of the Rue St. Antoine, in the timber-merchants' yards which then lay there, and with all the platforms and poles set up for the ceremony ; and they dedicated the engraving to the National Guards, whose day of glory it commemorated, and inscribed on it two verses of Béranger, and distributed copies to the drummer-boys to sell ; but the speculation was not, we are told, remunerative, for the drummer-boys used regularly to expend in drink every evening the receipts of the day. Trimolet was *always* an unlucky man !

In this year 1840, also, Daubigny took up seriously the study of etching; in the beginning he used regularly to plough down his copper plates, after he had taken a few prints of them, for economy's sake, and he made his work, done with needles for a burin, very minute and fine. In his etchings for the "Songs of France," M. Henriet adds : he passes "*des tons de roulette*, and makes skies *à la mécanique*," not to be unlike the rest of the book, but his dances, village festivals, and similar scenes are "jovial" and original in composition.

* His address this year is in the Salon catalogue, not at the social "phalanstère," but at 22, Rue de la Cerisaie. The landscape was a reminiscence of his walk into Italy—a view in the *Rampe des Commènes, Bourg d'Oisans, Department Isère.* Connoisseur M. Héricart de Thury wrote on an engraving of it that he perfectly recognised the mountains of Oisans, but the small trees in the picture were Parisian, not Alpine. An engraving of this picture is given in "L'Artiste" (Séries 2, Tome V.).

In this year, also, begins the celebrated fiasco of his competition for the landscape Prix de Rome ; he studied first for six months under Paul Delaroche, passed successfully through the stages called the " sketch en loge," and the "historic tree," and was one of the eight selected from these trials for the final competition. But he was ignorant of a rule that required his attendance at the schools on the day before the examination, and in his absence was disqualified. The prize was awarded to a man much older than himself, Hippolyte Lanoue, the subject of the trial picture being, according to Henriet, *Adam and Eve,* but according to other authorities, *Apollo Tending Sheep.*" *

The wheels grind slowly in labouring through the narrative of a life so overloaded with work as that of Daubigny, and the necessity of condensation adds to the difficulty of our task. The most superficial systematic review of the engraved work of this prolific genius would exceed our limits. M. Henriet divides his work into two distinct parts—the life of the painter, and that of the engraver. Daubigny himself did the same ; he made engraving the business of his life, by which he earned the means of supporting the painter, and he never allowed the painter to know the pressure of want, or to be influenced by considerations of the market. The engraver slaved that the painter might be free and independent ; he was a sort of little " phalanstère " to himself. In the few pages that we shall now devote to his career as a painter, we must remember that all his painting may be called "supererogation," and that he was working hard at the business of engraving, while he painted for his pleasure and ambition.

1841.—His failure in the competition for the Prix de Rome

* See Seubert's "Künstler Lexicon." The writer there speaks with considerable praise of Lanoue, whom Henriet appears to disparage.

THE MARSH. FROM THE ETCHING BY DAUBIGNY.

is the turning-point in his career. He refused the offer of
Delaroche to instruct him without remuneration, and betook
himself instead to the suburbs and fields about the *barrières* of
Paris, and now passed through that experience, common to so
many great landscape painters, of *thinking* that he threw off
like a snake's old skin, the influence of all that he had been
taught in the schools, and began a new life of spontaneous
appreciation of the lessons of Nature herself. Corot said the
same, and Rousseau, and how many more ! The *nation* said
the same, and they were the voice of it. Dr. Meyer * makes
a three-act drama of the movement in art that produced these
men at last. He begins with the period of the Restoration :
" Men were heartily tired," he says, "of the iron yoke in
which the irresistible hand of the Emperor had confined all the
relations, even of *intellectual* life . . . . . and, as the nation
shook off the fetters it had worn so long, and stretched its
limbs in liberty, *Art* also tried to break free from the trammels
in which the classic school had held it so long. One mastery
had gone hand in hand with the other, and renovated Art, for
a time at least, made common cause with the 'Life, Hope, and
Liberty,' expected from the advent of the new monarchy"
(hence the first, or Romantic period). "But this mood of
exaltation that welcomed the Bourbons passed away by their
own fault, and Art then sank down to the grade of a servile
interpretation of their policy." (This had been previously
defined to be the reconstruction of the broken links of the
chain of history, interrupted by the revolutionary and imperial
episodes.) "But the newly-awakened intellectual life of the
nation demanded a new style of Art; although, under the
political influences of the time, a wave of reaction passed in

* "History of Modern French Painting since 1789, in its Relation to
Political Life, Morals, and Literature."

the direction of classicism. Hence the second, or Classic-
Romantic period, directed chiefly to the memory of ancient
French history." Dr. Meyer remarks of this period that the
artists of it had no individuality, but were carried first in one
direction and then in another, with the stream of the Art
influences of the day, until with Géricault there appeared
"the young men of genius, strongly marked and decided
natures, who impelled Art into new channels by their own
force, and gave a clear and salient expression to the new views
that were darkly at work in the Spirit of the Age." These
men of independent genius are the founders of the Naturalistic
school, of which Géricault is regarded by Dr. Meyer as the
first apostle.

In landscape, the successors of Géricault, the men who "go
to Nature," are our Barbizon painters, and of them all the most
typical Naturalists, men who seek the truth of Nature for its
own sake, and for no by-ends of Impressionism, Romanticism
or beauty, are Dupré and Daubigny—par excellence Daubigny.
And in saying this, we remember that the quality of simple
truth—and nothing more—is not the highest, although, as the
world is, it is very high. We have some extracts from the
critics which explain our meaning, and Daubigny's right rank.
Henriet says: "Daubigny rendered all that he saw with a
simplicity of method, a naïveté of sentiment, an accuracy of
tone and emphasis which introduced a new element into landscape and opened the road to pure Naturalism. Henceforth,
the revolution that landscape had passed through with the first
generation of Romanticism—Paul Huet, Diaz, Dupré, Rousseau
—was accomplished. Seeking especially for dramatic expression in landscape, the Romantics had their pre-occupations,
their literary alloy to which Daubigny was insensible. They
were running after something in Nature other than Nature's

self; investing her with their personal thought; they were on the brink of a convention which was not indeed that of the Academy of Fine Arts, but none the less was the arbitrary creation of the Romantic group. Now, Daubigny would have no convention of any sort; he rejected altogether that Art of the learned, which can only be understood by the learned. He felt that Art should have a wider, more general scope; should speak to the hearts of the poor as well as the men of leisure and study; in a word, should be human. His means to this end were scrupulous fidelity, absolute respect for Nature, perfect and sincere personal disinterestedness." (This characteristic takes Daubigny—in his earlier style—out of the School called 'Impressionist.')

M. Théodore Pelloquet* says : "The manner of M. Daubigny, prodigiously simple and naïve, could never please, in the first instance, the enthusiasts for *ragouts* and for complex methods; but he is one of the most faithful and the most exact of interpreters of Nature. Nobody better than he gives to a landscape its just accent and its true character. By these very rare qualities he is of the family of the Masters; like them, he has the gift of breadth of execution, *primesautière* (spontaneous), without emphasis, but without hesitation. It is of him that one can say, 'he is a Realist,' if there be any meaning in the word. It is better to acknowledge that his painting is sincerity itself. A man must have lived in the closest intimacy with Nature to render in so striking a manner the most fugitive effects, the most daring harmonies. Endowed with an exquisite and profound feeling for local tone, he is not afraid to attack the reproduction of certain landscapes which the commonalty of painters would never dare to attempt; and he makes charming works of subjects in which many of his

* "Dictionnaire de poche des artistes contemporains, 1858."

colleagues, who pass for colourists, would have found nothing but a 'dish of spinach.' M. Daubigny is a painter throughout, and always. I know some vignettes, a few centimètres in size, drawn by him some ten or twelve years ago for railway guides, but executed with more breadth and mastery than many important and much-praised canvases. One word of criticism along with these praises (incomplete as they are). M. Daubigny is reproached that his pictures too often resemble studies. This blame, which is sometimes well founded, means that the painter, working from Nature, sometimes leaves in his work some parts incomplete of execution, in the fear that, if he finishes them, he may lose "that flower of *naïveté*, that sincerity of expression, which he esteems above everything else, and he does rightly."

Edmond About* devotes rather a longer paragraph than usual with him, to the praise of Daubigny's unassuming selection of subjects for his painting. "Poussin, and M. Desgoffe," he says, "are painters of Nature—M. Daubigny is, *par excellence*, the painter of the *campagne*," and distinguishes : "*Nature* conveys an idea of grandeur—*campagne* an idea of *bien-être intime et familier*. Grand outlines, vast plains, high mountain peaks, are of the domain of *Nature*, but—

> "Je sais sur la colline
> Une étroite maison ;
> Une tour la domine,
> Un buisson d'aubépine
> Est tout son horizon."

" *Voilà la campagne*, and M. Daubigny's Kingdom! His *Spring Loaded with Flowers* is a little masterpiece of impersonal painting ; the hand of man does not appear in it. In the landscapes of M. Desgoffe the hand makes its *power* felt, and in

---

* "Nos Artistes au Salon," 1857.

SPRINGTIME. BY DAUBIGNY. *In the Louvre.*

those of M. Corot its *delicacy*, but the work of M. Daubigny is like the smile of Spring seen through a window. This art without artifice or *parti pris* transports us bodily to the meadows and trees. This gamut of happy colours does not seem to have been found on a palette, but supplied by the sun himself. We have no intention of making a compliment to the artist when we wish we were a bird to perch on his branches, or a lizard to trot about hidden in the grass, or a grasshopper to nibble

> ' La fleurette
> Qui s'éveille aux baisers du vent
> Et rajuste sa collerette,
> Au miroir du soleil levant.' "

Dr. Julius Meyer devotes an appreciative review to Daubigny's paintings. He says it was not before the 50's that he reached to his full power, and the pictures of that time, of the picturesque suburbs of Paris, or of the Isère (Alpine), "give, with convincing truth, the first freshness of a simple nature-effect, in a rapid, *flowing* treatment, which does not yet quite suppress the detail. There is no attempt at powerful or unexpected effects, but only for the clear rendering of the moods, which the landscape itself brings with it for a receptive eye; and only for scenes that recur from day to day in quiet weather, the dewy cool of the morning or the quiet gentle air of noon. In this style are the *Harvest* of 1852, a *View of the Banks of the Seine* and the *Pool of Gylien* of 1853." Other critics objected to the *Harvest*—which is a brilliant painting with many figures, teams of horses, haymakers, waggoners, &c.—that the drawing was sacrificed to the general effect; that it was a splendid sketch, not a finished work. There is an etching of it, dated 1862, which certainly shows nothing of the details of the picture. But in the *Pool*

of Gylien, Daubigny is at his best. The Comte Clément de Ris
writes, in *L'Artiste* of 15 June, 1853, quite an idyll about it—
" calm, restful, full of forms that are elegant and peaceful, of
colours unobtrusive and harmonious, of softened lights and
shadows," where " the poetical silence seemed to have always
ruled unbroken. A lake, set like a mirror among the gentle-
browed hills, and the rims of the cup are decorated with
sheaves of rushes, of tussilage, of reeds, and *fraisiers d'eau*, and
the surface with white and yellow leaves of the water-lily
on which a world of flies and other insects hum." He calls
it a picture that you can inhale, as well as see, and says
there emanates from it an aroma of wet leaves, which
intoxicates (*énivre*) you ! Sleeping water is a speciality with
Daubigny.

" As Daubigny advanced," Dr. Meyer goes on to say, " he
quickly acquired that freedom of treatment which is characteristic of all his work, and, in his best time, is remarkably
skilful, without any mannerism, in the expression of a quiet,
subdued Nature-harmony in light and air. His choice of subject also is still characterized by a naïve simplicity. The scene
that he still loves to paint, is always a cheerful piece of undu-
lating land, full of foliage, on meadow lands, or by the banks
of bright mirrors of streams, with a light grey, misty cloud-
play over it, such as the North so constantly exhibits in mild
weather. Often he seems to have no other object than the
mere copying of such a landscape. But he lets the mist-veiled
sunlight streak the river and the grass, the warm spring breeze
fan through the trees ; he saturates form and colour with the
tender breath of the atmosphere, and so makes us all share
equally the sentiment that he himself receives from Nature
and her moods, in the glow of noon or in the silence of
evening. So, for example, the full brilliance of the day is

LANDSCAPE. BY DAUBIGNY.

poured out, in 'einheitlichem Ton,' with still stronger local colour, over the *Lock Gate in the Valley of Optevoz,** a picture of most cheerful, peaceful tone, even in the shadows of the *beneficent* (kindly "wohlthuender") freshness and brightness." M. Henriet finds this picture *un peu noyée*, in spite of the exquisite tones of it. "It gives you the fresh sensation of inhaling a bouffée of air and light."

Dr. Meyer goes on, "The '*durchschlagende*' success that he had in the Salon of 1857 made Daubigny the leader of the Realistic school. Of his pictures of that year, the *Spring* is in the Luxembourg ; † it represents nothing more than a field of corn, still green in the blade, extending far and wide in the background, and some apple-trees in blossom. But the tone of the land-surface in the distance is so happily graduated, the green in the white meridian light is so soft, and shimmering and fresh, that the eye is attracted '*tief hinein,*' and you feel a longing to walk there full of pleasant thought.

"His pictures of 1859 also, and among them, especially, the *Banks of the Oise*, still show the same innocent charm. But already the *sketchiness* of his work gets beyond all bounds. There is still some excuse for it, while the form of objects is indicated by the fine graduation of *tones*, but all detail is merged in shapeless masses by the treatment in broad spread tints, often only lightly rubbed in.

"In recent years Daubigny has gone still further in this direction. Now he keeps only *one* distinct, combined effect in view, which is to strike the spectator as *one* full, strong tone. Now, too, he looks about for *impressions*, which, however abundant they may be in Nature, have scarcely ever yet found their entrance into painting, and he often selects, with this object in view, a *cutting* from Nature absolutely un-beautiful,

* 1855. In the Luxembourg.   † Now in the Louvre.

which would never tempt a traveller to linger on his way. A herd of sheep on a stony stubble-field at the fall of night, a miserable village on the overhanging bank of a dirty brook, late in the evening twilight (both of 1861). A moonlight shining through dark clouds on a barren heath with two hovels upon it (1865); landscapes which are made to produce effect only by their power of tone, and energy of the general impression, and do not miss the production of this effect on one looking at them from a distance, but closely inspected appear to be nothing but an indistinguishable mass of strokes of the brush, laid oilily and broadly on the canvas. But, in the meantime, from time to time, the painter comes back to a *friendlier* nature, especially to the green banks of the Oise, where the round, thick-foliaged trees are reflected on the placid waters, and over the rich fertile meadows the repose of the light summer air is lying. Such impressions, the reflection of a Nature full of light and colour, Daubigny still knows how to communicate, even yet, although his handling of his subjects drowns form and shape so much." The above is far the most impressive valuation of Daubigny's work that I have found. Dr. Meyer goes on to that of his successors, beginning with the words :— "There is no one of the others who comes up to Daubigny," and then mentions Charles Leroux, Charles Busson, Léon Ville-ville, Adolphe Appian, Eugène Lavieille (a Barbizon painter), Emile Lambinet, and many others, as the scholars in Daubigny's school, for Daubigny must undoubtedly be regarded as the founder of a school, which promises to be permanent and predominant in landscape art.

Reverting now to our narrative of the incidents of his biography, and to the year 1841, when he entered upon that phase of life which so many men of genius think peculiar to themselves, and shaking off the authority of the schools (which had, however, done their part in his apprenticeship) began to look at landscape with a Master's independence, we find that the first result of his new ambition is an increase of industry in the humbler duties on which he depended. "The number of vignettes that he drew at that time," M. Henriet says, "is inconceivable for the various publishers who employed him: Curmer, Ernest Bourdin, Delloye, Hetzel, Furne, Hachette, &c." Scarcely an illustrated book came out, but he had a hand in it; he poured out *croquis à la plume*, and *lavis sur pierre* frantically.

At the same time he must have been working on his etchings like a student who had no other occupation in life, and those who would make a thorough study of his genius should by no means neglect this branch of its development, in which so many impressions find expression which the painter despairs of rendering with the brush. In the Salons of 1841 and 1845 he showed a frame of etchings, mostly souvenirs of the Dauphine, of Morvan, or the îles Bezons—lazy waters, flowing soothingly among beds of water-lilies, overshadowed by trees on the banks—silent woods, and solitary paths, and happy lovers wandering there in couples—pale and *half-warm* April days with merry birds singing on the branches—orchards in the blossom of Spring—these were the dreams of Daubigny—the incessant worker, the waking dreamer—the rough-mannered, loud-voiced, tender poet—the boisterous, athletic boating-man!

The accidents of his history lose their interest by the side of the study of his character. This is felt by his biographers who have not put them on record. He was happy in his art, in his family, in his own temperament. He travelled a great deal. The sketches with which his studio was encumbered

From a photograph by M. Georges Petit.]   ON THE OISE. BY DAUBIGNY.

bear record of innumerable excursions of which the history is lost;—flat shores at low water, seaweed harvests, fleets of fishing boats, from his numerous visits to the coasts of Brittany and Normandy—reminiscences of Morvan, of la Bresse, of Picardy—foggy Thames scenery, from his English tour of 1866 —canals and mills of Holland, from a journey he made with his son Karl, in 1871—posadas and streets of Spanish towns, from a journey with Henri Regnault, in 1868—the studio was like a warehouse, full of pictures, pictures heaped up in the corners, pictures on the walls, pictures unfinished on the easels; but it showed not another ornament at all—everything in it was directed to Work. As Henriet says: "Le luxe capital de Daubigny, ce sont tout bonnement les peintures de Daubigny!"

It was in 1859 that he built himself the celebrated ark of a boat that he christened *le Botin*,* and became the sworn painter of the riverside, as he drifted down the stream from the Ile-Adam to Conflans, from Conflans to Bonnières, to Andelys, and so on to the Pont de l' Arche, stopping to paint here and there, as the fancy seized him. He took his young son Karl with him on these excursions, and trained him to such purpose that he began life at seventeen, the exhibitor of two landscapes, taken at Auvers, in the Salon of 1863.

He decorated his boat himself. Henriet tells of his calling to him: "Come along with me, I am going to paint the 'Botin.'" And when they reached the riverside, and Henriet expected to be shown another *Bord de l'Oise*, it was not a picture but the old boat itself that Daubigny was painting.

In 1868 he built himself a house at Auvers, on a spot where

---

* Or, as Yriarte says, *le Bottin*. I can find in Littré or elsewhere no explanation of this name. Possibly it refers to the "Bottin," or Paris Directory, a fat, bulky volume.

he had often camped out with his family in previous summers. Oudinot was its architect. Corot, son Karl and Oudinot, but principally Daubigny himself, decorated it. M. Charles Yriarte described it in *Le Monde Illustré* (27 June, 1868) :—

"Daubigny, who is indebted to the banks of the Oise for his finest triumphs, has built for himself *la Maison du Sage* at Auvers, a little above Pontoise, in a charming village on the slope of a hill, a village where thatched roofs are not extinct. The place has only one street, but what a street it is! It stretches out in one straight line, and it is a league in length.

"The full, broad Oise flows at two paces away, with real *cliffs*, which are the delight of the *paysagistes*—cliffs where the big rushes and willows are growing free—where washerwomen and anglers flourish, where the eddies eat grey wounds in the green banks, careless of the straight line, and picturesque unexpectedly.

"The île de Vaux parts the bed of the river in two, and great carpets of water-lilies make the foreground to these ready-made pictures, in front of which the painter has nothing to do but to sit down with his umbrella planted in the ground and his box of colours on his knees.

"Daubigny's boat, the *Bottin*, is his peripatetic studio. How many rivers has it seen, that *Bottin!* Sometimes rowed, sometimes towed, shaving the banks and bending the long reeds under its prow! The *Bottin* has grown old at last, and retires on the sick-list, and his cabin will be a refuge for the ladies who wish to bathe under the willows. The master, Daubigny, is building himself a new boat.

"The house at Auvers is simple and unpretending, but there is a grain of caprice in it—a caprice that a prince of the blood royal could scarcely afford. In the broad lobby Corot has painted some frescoes for his friend ; in one, one of those bits of dreamland that he excels in, a Virgilian land-scape, a corner of the Vale of Tempé. A mountain torrent washes the base of a woody knoll, large and noble trees slope down towards the water, a bather clings to the tendrils and regains the bank. It is Baia or Tivoli, but we are sure it is Corot. . . . . Then Daumier, a great artist also, has painted Don Quixote and his faithful squire, in a deep gorge, marching on to victory. In the foreground the carcase of a Rosinante is drawn, with that knowledge of osteology and that *grand jet de dessin* which are Daumier's mastery. Near to Daumier, Oudinot, who was Daubigny's architect, has painted a fresh landscape. . . . . The dining-room is simpler; it is divided into panels, and on each of them Daubigny himself has painted attributes and bits of nature. The most original of these panels represents *Angling*. Imagine the mirage of the water, the cork float with its red point and its quill, the line which describes a profile against the sky, then the ' *coupe de l'eau*' ;—that is to say, the mystery of the aquarium, that which passes round the hook when ' there is a bite !' The little silver gudgeons twist themselves about and dally with the red worm, bleak and sticklebacks look at the bait distrustfully, all that life swarms and moves about the prey with pearly reflections, and in the dark, green background the slow-moving carp, the eels, the barbel, and the tench are sleeping.

"The bedroom of his daughter Daubigny has painted throughout in fresco, with that real poetry—simple and unaffected—of an artist reared in the great school of nature. The subjects are exquisite in lustre.

"The wall at the foot of the bed he has covered with branches of may in blossom and nests of little singing-birds. It is the song of the Spring: the great white blossoms open, the hawthorn twines, the newly-hatched birds stretch out their yellow beaks. . . . . On the panels little Tom Thumb is sowing his breadcrumbs, whilst his brothers vanish in the wood. Red Riding Hood is talking to the wolf; and there are attributes—children's toys, dolls with rosy cheeks, the 'toctoc' mallet, little yellow windmills, paper dogs that squeak; and then girls' toys—la grace, shuttlecock, rackets, butterfly net; and round it all, as a frame, there are wreaths—wreaths of white roses, of red roses, of corn-flowers, of daisies, of violets, of pansies, of tuberoses, fresh lilac, red cherries that the children wear for earrings, wreath of field flowers, poppies, and ears of corn for harvest-home.''

In the above description of his house, one seems to have the whole man, better portrayed than he would be by the most careful analysis of character.

One word more to the Art critic on the subject of the change that came to his pictures in 1861, when they became careless in execution, confused in detail, but directed to a unity of expression, "an impressionist dream." *Le Parc à Moutons, Le Lever de Soleil*, of this year are the first notes of this new key, and deserve close study and comparison with his other simul-

he did not vacillate to and fro, as others did (Rousseau, for example) and as Henriet says, "he passed through no crisis nor transformations," with the one exception of the change in this year 1861, "when the line of his *tableaux clairs* comes to an end."

He was nominated to the Legion of Honour, in the year of his great success with the *Spring*, and the *Valley of Optevoz*, in 1857. In 1874, after the Vienna exhibition, he was promoted Officier.

Henriet says he was the first painter who ever finished a large picture entirely in the open air.

This was the case with his Salon picture of 1864, *Viller-ville sur mer*, when he fixed his canvas on to substantial posts set in the ground, and kept it there *en permanence*, exposed "to the horns of the ruminants and the tricks of the boys," until he had finished it. He had put in a sky, "Gris mouvementé," with great clouds driving across it before the wind, and used to stand at the window for hours, watching for the favourable moment, and run out to work on it as soon as the weather took the effect aimed at in the picture. M. Henriet adds that this was the more praiseworthy because Daubigny was subject to rheumatism.

Daubigny died at Paris, on the 19th of February, 1878. M. Henriet, writing in 1881, says: "Death, during the last few years, has reaped a large harvest from the ranks of our landscape painters. She has struck down, before their time, valiant soldiers : Daliphart, Marcellin de Groizeillez, Herpin. She has taken our generals Th. Rousseau, Chintreuil, Millet, Corot and DAUBIGNY, the most popular, if not the greatest of them all."

From a photograph by M. Georges Petit.]

COAST SCENE. BY DUPRÉ.

JULES DUPRÉ.

ONE of the most celebrated art-critics of France, M. Ernest
Chesneau, describes the type of landscape that he re-
gards as classical, "without a touch of nature, where skies,
trees, rocks and water, are copied from an appointed model,
so false and so simple as to excite a smile if it were an
individual example, but a thing to be troubled for as a
collective example or the law of a school." From this, he
goes on to say, "the romantic landscape is not a reaction, but
a transition"—whose representative painters "did not flinch
from selecting, correcting, and in case of need adding or re-
trenching. Simple nature did not strike them as rich enough
in *accident*, in extraordinary phenomena, and they, the
Romanticists, supplied the want." The new departure is regarded in many ways, by different writers, each from his own
point of view, few agreeing or writing from similar standing
points. The following is from Luebke's "History of Art":—
"A few artists follow that ideal style which seeks the beauty of
landscape in the plastic development of outline; like Paul
Flandrin, Hippolyte Lanoue, Louis Français, and above all
Corot, with his pictures enveloped in a silvery haze. The
greater number reject all richness of outline, and turn all their
powers to the reflection of atmospheric effects and conditions
of light, amid the simplest scenery, and in simple everyday

truth; though masters, like Daubigny, Théodore Rousseau, and Jules Dupré, have attained to a height of effect in this direction which, acting like a charm upon the unadorned portrayal of nature in her homeliest aspects, invests it with a true poetic feeling." The distinction between the Impressionists and the true classics is rather succinctly drawn by M. Chesneau, who says: "The highest school in art is that which is for ever guided towards the beautiful ideal. A lower school is that which is contented to create a record of *impressions* received. They are the school of sensation, of which *Rubens is the type.* To distinguish the two schools, label their frontispieces respectively *Le beau dans l'esprit,* and *Le beau dans la nature.*"

Against which one may quote Littré: "Tout réel n'est pas beau, mais il n'y a de beau, même idéal, que dans le réel."

With reference to the practice of the Romantic school of sending for exhibition paintings that were rather sketches than finished work, and of sacrificing composition and design to colour, the former class were stigmatised as *pochades* and the latter as *tartouillades.* M. Delécluze, reviewing the "Exhibition of the Works of Living Artists," made at Paris in 1850, says: "In spite of the natural and reasonable disgust that I am inspired with by productions which can only be properly characterized by words as disgusting as themselves, necessity obliges me to enter into some detail in respect of the *tartouillades* —of the *pochades*—of all those *undigested* paintings whose troublesome vicinity obscures the brilliance of the works of value contained in the exhibition." Among the "men of 1830," Rousseau appears the only one who, in his later years, was influenced by such criticisms as the above to adopt extreme finish: "Un art fini jusqu'à la mesquinerie," as M. Woolff calls it.

Jules Dupré is called by many French writers the father of

the Barbizon school, but this is not the same thing as the founder of the school of romantic landscape, or of the "Impressionist" school attributed to Géricault. Moreover there is reason in the conjecture that the liberation of landscape originated in England. "The genius of Constable," says a writer in *L'Art*, "exercised a powerful influence upon French painters of thirty years ago, and the talented group of men who drew their inspiration from his art have left a lasting impression upon the work of their successors." The salient characteristics of Constable, "exaggeration of unity and singleness of impression, and neglect of *imitative* reality," might be predicated of Corot ; as well as that other minor characteristic of *moistness*, of which Mrs. Jameson* tells the old anecdote, mentioning Constable's "splashy, showery effect on foliage, and cool airy sky." She says, "We can hardly look on his pictures without feeling that there is some truth in Fuseli's sarcasm : 'I go to visit Constable. Bring me mine ombrella ! '"

But no patriotic French critic will admit the English origin of the "renaissance in miniature." M. Albert Woolff attributes it to Rousseau. "English landscape painters of the date of the Restoration," he admits, "also revolted from the historic landscape, but their works were unknown in France " (Rousseau, however, was hung upon one occasion between a Constable and a Bonington), "and the renaissance in France was independent, and Rousseau was at the head of it."

But ·if Rousseau was at the head of it, *à fortiori* so was Dupré, the teacher of Rousseau. Jules Clarétie says of him : "Jules Dupré belongs to that generation of landscape painters which immediately followed Michallon, and burned the temple of Style to raise an altar to Nature. It may be that the Eng-

* " Handbook to the National Gallery."

lish landscape painters—the Boningtons, the Turners, the Constables—were not foreigners to this movement, which drew in their train our own artists after them, Rousseau, Troyon, Flers, Daubigny." Paul Mantz writes, retrospectively, in 1867 :—"We remember what his part was in those first hours, when it was necessary to restore to landscape painting, the prey of the Academicians, its liberty, its truth, its colour. M. Dupré was admirable in those contests which had for object, and for result, the deliverance of captive Nature."

To arrive at Jules Dupré, to place him in the history of modern landscape, a retrospect is indispensable. He is preceded immediately by Paul Huet (b. 1804) and by Charles de Laberge (1807-1842) ; by Camille Flers (b. 1802) and by Louis Cabat, the pupil of Flers and the friend of the boyhood of Dupré—and his mission was to strike the *juste milieu* of this epoch-making group. All these painters "went to Nature" as frankly as Dupré himself, but their efforts were tentative, experimental, and their idiosyncrasies strongly - marked ; Dupré resuméd them, and was regarded as the founder of a school.

HUET sought the subjective impression of a landscape, and neglected or merged into the whole his detail; he was afraid of light, and his pictures are dull, but full of poetry. Poor LABERGE lost himself in detail—"He would make thirty sketches of a thistle for an obscure corner of his foreground, and built up a wall in his studio to study the tone of each brick by itself," but, in spite of this, he brought the whole into harmony and expression of feeling ; notably in a *Sunset*, now to be seen in the Louvre, a dark group of oaks on the skirts of an open hill country, in which, in spite of the minute elaboration of every leaf, the whole impression of the peace and quiet of a warm evening twilight is beautifully expressed.

THE PUNT. BY JULES DUPRÉ.

FLERS produced no perfect pictures, but his sympathy was with the new method of a frank study of nature; he painted Nature in her Sunday dress, every-day nature glorified with light and light effects.

His pupil, CABAT, took a more important position, and, no doubt, from his intimacy in youth with Jules Dupré, influenced the latter materially. He is, in effect, the true pioneer of the "men of 1830"; and it·is attributable to the exigencies of the Market that he has been thrown into the background of late years: "Inspired by the study of the Dutch masters, his practice was to take a common piece of the nearest 'domestic' nature (*der nächsten heimischen Natur*), frankly and plainly, for the subject of his picture, and then he made it his business to reproduce the separate parts of it (*das Einzelne*) in form, as well as in tone (without binding himself slavishly to the detail, like ·Laberge) with fidelity, and, at the same time, to attain the effect of the whole composition, the 'elementary' impression that pervaded the whole,*—and he succeeded. But, later in life, in consequence of a voyage to Italy, he changed his style; and, although we have not space to analyse it, the story of the gradual influence of the Italian sky upon this student of the atmospheric effects of our different latitudes is full of instruction and interest to the rational student of the history of landscape art. It was in his early period that he influenced Dupré and was regarded as the leader of the Romantic school in landscape.

Jules Dupré was born at *Nantes* in 1812 :—"His father had

---

* "Ihm war es darum zu'thun, das Einzelne in der Form sowol wie im Ton, ohne dasz er sich sklavisch wie de Laberge an das Detail band, treu wiederzugeben und doch die einheitliche Stimmung zu treffen."— *Meyer.*

a china-shop at Nantes, where Jules was born," the *Times* says, on the occasion of the announcement of his death, on the 8th of October, 1889. "M. Jules Dupré was born in 1812 at *Île-Adam*," M. Réné Ménard says, in the biographical sketch that he wrote on the same occasion for *L'Art*.

"He was born at Nantes in 1811," (!) says M. Jules Claretie, "He is the son of a manufacturer of porcelain whose name is one of the oldest of the little village of Parmain, which is opposite to Île-Adam."*

Wherever he was born, we cannot doubt that his childhood and youth passed at Île-Adam. "His *brother* desired to entrust him some day with the management of his manufactory of porcelain; and in his youth he prepared himself with docility for this career."†

"He followed at first his *father's* calling as a porcelain manufacturer."‡

"His early education was shortened. He was very young when he was apprenticed, because it was necessary to place him promptly in a position to gain his own living; but, as he had a very decided taste for art, he was put with Diébold, "ancien peintre raté," who had never been worth anything as an artist, and had retired to Île-Adam, and was a "peintre de pendules."§ His occupation was to paint round a Brobdingnag clock-face a landscape of Lilliput, with a clock-turret, leaving a round hole for the face to show. "These clocks," M. Ménard

* The little village of Parmain was distinguished in the war of 1870 by an exploit of its citizen *francs-tireurs*, in revenge of which it was burnt to the ground, and some citizens were shot, by sentence of court-martial, by the Germans.

† Larousse, *Dic. Universelle du XIX. Siècle, s.v.*

‡ Meyer, Konversations-lexikon, *s.v.*

§ Réné Ménard.

says, "are sold cheaper than those that have no pictures, because they are fitted with inferior works, and they are cheaper than pictures without clocks, because the painters of this kind of landscape are poorly paid."

We assume that Dupré was first apprenticed to the porcelain works, and thence transferred to the clock painting; also that the porcelain works were those of his brother, or his father, or (some writers say) his uncle; and, further, that they were the same works at which Diaz, Cabat, and other young painters were working at the same time. It is to be remembered, also, that Daubigny also found work at this time at "tableaux pendules."

After a time, M. Ménard says, Dupré was enabled to come to Paris, and there he met Cabat, whom he had known as a boy, —who was precisely his own age,—and was an apprentice,— but found leisure to study the old masters in the Louvre; and, in effect, when Dupré met with him he was engaged in making a copy of a landscape of Isaak van Ostade.—Whether this was before or after the time when Cabat became the pupil of Flers we are not informed.—He showed Dupré over the Louvre, and Dupré resolved then and there to become a landscape painter, and to work from Nature. He was, we are told, at this time thrown on his own resources, and without friends. This is, however, strikingly improbable, although, no doubt, he became one of that band of *enfants trouvés* of Painting whom M. Charles Clement described :—

"There lived at that time, outside of the studios, in the dark haunts of the ouvrier class at Paris, some young men of sixteen or twenty years of age, the sons of artisans for the most part, enamellers, decorators, designers of patterns on stuffs or on porcelain, daubers of signs for shops—who all went every

F

Sunday to the Louvre, and to the *banlieue* of Paris, as if by a sort of instinct, and strolled along the banks of the Seine *up* to Charenton and *down* to Neuilly—inquisitive, dreamy, eager to see and to learn—much as Poussin, whom they owned for their master, had gone about dreaming, in his time, in the suburbs of Rome.

"On Monday they returned to the work of real life, and began to draw on the bottoms of plates the views they had seen on their holiday rambles. The repetition of this engraved the landscapes on their memories, which grew into pictures later on.

"They used to make a few sketches from nature, very slight and fugitive—towing-paths, trampled by the horses, winding, stony, and bordered with short and dusty grass on the side towards the land, and by sand, damp, *défoncé*, and mingled with great herbs on the side of the water; or a stranded boat moored to the stump of a willow-tree; or an angler motionless, watching his float; or a watering-place of cattle in a creek, and horses going down to it—horses of *three* colours: white, black, and red—and the driver of them always in a straw hat and a blue blouse, mounted on the white horse; or factory chimneys emitting smoke in vaster horizons; or tall cranes on wheels, which revolve on the tops of stone quarries and embankments, &c. The sky in these pictures is grey; the perspective open, over a flat country, and the fields of clover, and of poor crops in a corner, where a few cows are grazing, and the grey donkey of Karel Dujardin.

"Behold the first steps in contemporary landscape! That is the way in which all of them began—Cabat, Dupré, Flers, Diaz, and the others."

M. Ménard's narrative proceeds to tell how Dupré sold some

of his studies to a man who sold curiosities of all sorts in the
streets, and supported himself by this means until he met with
a remarkable, ideal *patron* in a Marquis, who not only bought all
the stock-in-trade that he had in sketches, but ordered a
picture—a landscape, with figures—with the stipulation that
the figures were not to be *personnages*, such as pupils of a
classical master would introduce, but real live *bonshommes*, such
as he, being a sportsman, was accustomed to see going about in
the country.

Other amateurs, M. Ménard says, followed the Marquis, and
Dupré's success, and with it the *renaissance* in landscape, of
which he was the principal agent, was secure.

In place of all this, it is open to us to suppose that Dupré's
relations, having consented to his adoption of the profession of
art, supported the boy from their sufficient means, whilst he was
devoting his energies to the study of nature which resulted in
his succesful *début* at the age of nineteen in the Salon of 1831
with those views of Haute-Vienne, Île-Adam, and Mont-
morency, which the critic, Lenormant, seized at once: as
"calm and peaceful pastures," "an art healthy and attractive
as the memory of our peasant nurses,"—comparing them
with Rousseau's portrayal of "les forces les plus sauvages
de la nature."

The Salon of 1831, says M. Alfred Sensier, saw the "entrée
en campagne" of a new school, and all the recruits were
there: Eugène Delacroix with his *Liberty;* Scheffer with his
first *Faust;* Roquelin with twelve pictures; Eugène Lami,
Jeanron, Deveria, Poterlet, Johannot, Colin, Flers, Jules
André, Decamps, Diaz, Barye, were all there. Sensier says
that Dupré was at Boulogne-sur-Mer when he sent his first contribution to the Salon,—four beautiful landscapes of different

characters. . . . He had no party spirit; he was essentially a man of peace. He did not, indeed, introduce fresh life into the art world when he led the way into pastures, farms, and fields, the quiet forest or the peasant hut; but his compositions are always quiet and pastoral pictures of the peace of a country life.

"His cows chewing the cud, his horses grazing, with fluttering manes, among the fat herbage, all dwell in pleasant pastures and at peace with man. His was a wholesome and an attractive art, that seemed to fill the mind with memories of our peasant nurses." (The "peasant nurses," it will be observed, Sensier has borrowed, verbally, from M. Lenormant.)

Again in 1833, the great year of Rousseau's *Côtes de Granville*, Dupré took his station in the ranks of the combatant regenerators of landscape, "with Cabat, Flers, Jules André, Jadin, Roqueplan, Paul Huet, finally Diaz and Marilhat," says Sensier, and won praise from M. Lenormant, who said: "His landscape, with a hedge in the middle, although borrowed from recollection of Carl Dujardin, shows such an accuracy of *touch* in the foliage, so rich and so powerful a method of modelling the plans, so happy an arrangement of the light, that we are inclined to yield altogether to hope." The picture was very badly hung.

Dupré spent some years of his youth in England, and brought to the Salon, in 1836, a *Vue d'Angleterre*, of which the critic in the *Révue de Paris* says: "It is a true English meadow, diapered with tones as green and crude as malachite; still moistened with dew drops; and the solitude of it is *embroidered* with great shadows. Besides one *Battle Scene*, composed in partnership with M. Eugène Lami, this is all that M. Dupré shows us this year." Another work of his youth, exhibited in 1844, in the Galerie des Beaux Arts, is men-

tioned in the *Bulletin des Amis des Arts*, of that year, proba-
bly by Thoré (?), who says that it " belongs to the first series
of the works of his youth, and is his first step outside of the
painting taught by the Valenciennes, the Bidaults, and the
Victor Bertins, and finally modified by Michallon. We find in
it the ambition of an artist ready to break scholastic fetters
and to turn his attention to the masterworks of Huysman
and Ruysdael." The picture represented the *Interior of a
Forest*.

It is impossible to give a sketch of Dupré's life without
referring to Rousseau. M. Alfred Sensier describes a visit
that he made to the two friends about the year 1846, in their
house on the Place Pigalle, in which his opinion of their indi-
vidualities is laid very graphically before us.

He describes himself as returning from Rousseau, "brisé
de fatigue," with just strength left to go to bed—dreaming
all night of mountains, dark precipices, furious torrents, and
chaos.

" It was only with day-light," he says, "that calm came to
me, and that I understood Rousseau and his work. . . . .
Dupré had revealed to me the meaning of pastoral and rural
landscape in all its beauty and peace ; Rousseau unveiled the
world of past ages and the regions of tempest." The paintings of Dupré which Sensier had in his mind were drawings of
La Creuse and Berry.

Rousseau spent the spring of 1834 in preparations for a
journey to Switzerland. It was Jules Dupré who proved such
a counter-attraction that he hesitated on the eve of departure.
Rousseau did not wish to do without the society of Dupré, but
the latter's tastes led him to prefer the pastures of Limousin
and Berry to Switzerland. Rousseau, however, clung to his

plan. "He wanted to be near to the clouds, to contemplate
the regions of the tempest." However, it was Dupré whose
persuasive powers gained the day, and who, after trying to
drag Rousseau away with him to the borders of the Bousane
and the Vienne, succeeded in eliciting a promise from Rousseau
that he would join him at Les Marches and La Creuse.

We learn from Sensier, quite incidentally, the futility of all
that is said of Dupré's struggle, at any period of his career,
with any degree of poverty.

Already, in 1833—that is to say, *two years* only after his
début in the Salon, and in his twenty-first year—he is inviting
Rousseau to long excursions in the Dauphiné, and yet further
afield. In 1840—or sooner—it is Dupré who entertains the
club of the refractory painters at his lodgings in the Avenue
Trochot, which are good enough to accommodate—*so Sensier
says*—such men as Ary Scheffer, Décamps, Delacroix, Barye,
and Chenavart—but this is incredible. At least the suggestion
is enough to dissipate fables of impecuniosity on Dupré's side,
and the long catalogue of instances of his disinterested and
badly rewarded friendly offices for Rousseau begins.

It is shown almost as much by the retirement of the two
together to the little village of Monsoult, on the skirts of the
forest of Île-Adam, " near the family of Dupré—a charming
valley—dotted with orchards, rural plantations, &c."

In 1841 we find Mdme. Dupré, the mother of Jules, pre-
siding over a household of which the three members were
herself, Jules Dupré, and Rousseau, and Rousseau and Dupré
had their studios side by side.

In 1843 their intimacy was such that Sensier, alluding to
them as the " frères jumeaux," tells us that they were "in
the habit of refusing any invitations that excluded either of
them—and in this year they planned the journey into Gascony,

THE POOL. BY JULES DUPRÉ   In the Collection of A. H. Talmadge, Esq.

described in our biography of Rousseau, out of which Rousseau brought that " despair " of the faultless blue sky, which may have been accountable in later years, in part, for his *Japanese* eccentricities. Dupré, a more solid character, sketched, in his own style, the subjects they found, and his career is unmarked by any critical change at all. He was the most unselfish of friends, and in the long struggle, the universal animosity which lasted thirteen years, and was settled in the year 1848 by the fusilade of the Revolution; his preoccupation was of jealousy on behalf of Rousseau, who was excluded from the Salon all those years. His own interest in the education of the public taste was feeble, and when he had not the motive of serving Rousseau, he took no part in the discussions of the day. But the Revolution of 1848, which was the triumph of the "phalanx of déterminés,"* placed him and Rousseau on the Jury, which was elected on the new system, and a free distribution of honours fell to the friends of Thoré. Dupré received the cross of the Legion of Honour; but, to the astonishment of all the world, Rousseau did not. The reason of this neglect of him by his own partisans is unexplained. He visited his disappointment on Dupré, and as he persisted in the quarrel a coolness ensued between them. Dupré, a silent man, retired from public life, and desisted from exhibiting if not from painting, for a number of years.

Taking up his work again, after a lapse of years, in 1852, the critics seem to detect a change in his method. M. Planché says of the three pictures that he sent to the Salon of that year, "One of them deserves much praise, the smallest, with a marsh in the foreground ; but he, like

* Ricourt, Dupré, Lorentz, Diaz, Laviron, Décamps, Louis Boulanger, Gigoux, Garbet, Préault, Haussard, Jéhan Duseigneur, Landon, and some others, are mentioned under this name by a contemporary writer.

Rousseau, is growing *too precise*. '*Le mieux est quelquefois l'ennemi du bien.*'" He abstained from exhibiting for a number of years, and the alteration of his style increased.

In 1867 he sent in two pictures, *La Vanne* (the Sluice Gate) and the *Passage of Animals over a Bridge*, in the choice of which he was said to have wished to invite a comparison between his old manner and his new. *La Vanne*, M. Paul Mantz esteems " one of his masterpieces of old times. It is impossible to paint with greater vigour, to give better expression to the silence of the solitudes, or to colour with more energy the reeds, and alder trees, and shrubs which plunge their roots in the water and draw from it sap and life. To our feeling, *La Vanne* is one of the most beautiful landscapes of the modern school, one of those significant pages which mark an epoch, and which Museums will be fighting to possess some day. The other pictures exhibited belong to his new manner. Let us speak it out frankly ; they are not so beautiful as those of other times. There is a lively accent of colour in the *Passage of Animals over a Bridge*, and in another canvas of recent execution ; but in general the later landscapes of M. Dupré are of an execution a little heavy, and of a handling in which excessive impasto injures the transparency of the water, and the clearness of the skies. The trees freely affect tints of red or yellow, which seem to be systematic ; M. Dupré can no longer find on his palette those bold greens, those intense and powerful blues, which have been the delight of our youth. Perhaps the noble artist has done wrong to retire to solitude. Truly, to remain courageously in the *melée* is to be exposed to wounds, but it is to run the chance, also, of growing great."

After this year, it is said : " M. Jules Dupré is almost an

exile at Isle-Adam, where he works," and it is not until 1873 that he reappears, and M. Clarétie writes : "It is twenty years since the critics have been reproaching M. Dupré for not exhibiting. Those who forget themselves become readily forgotten, and I am not sure that everybody is now aware that the name I have just written is that of a master." The formation of clouds, the phenomena of the weather and of light, are the subjects in the treatment of which M. Dupré particularly excelled, and, it was said by many, surpassed any living painter of his period. There can be no doubt in any mind that the school, whatever it was, that he belonged to, was the *right* school; whether or not it was what enthusiasts in the matter understand by the Barbizon school, is altogether a different question—a question which reminds us of the quotation already used : "There is nothing so mischievous in the world, as Fashion in the Arts."

The work of Dupré is not inaptly paired with that of DAUBIGNY, whom, however, we must be permitted to think, he greatly excelled in original genius—but not, for it would be impossible, in conscientious industry, simplicity, and sincerity. The pity of it seems to be that two such painters should be thrust to *pose* before the world as the inventors of some new thing, and linked with the eccentric Rousseau !

"Dupré loves to paint the scenery of Western France, where barren hillocks, low-lying plains overgrown with heather, stagnant pools of water and ragged shrubs are found at the base of the rocky mountains. Sometimes he shows us cattle in a meadow near a wood, sleeping under an oak, or wading through a shallow ford ; at other times, some dreary and desolate hovel under the lea of wind-tossed trees ; or he leads us across a sunburnt common, by the side of a bit of forest, towards the deserted village, when the atmosphere overhead is dry and oppressive in the heats of midsummer. He is always true in his rendering of the atmosphere, of the cooling moisture in it that rises from saturated vegetation after a storm, or the sultry glare of drought, or the dance of a sunbeam, or drift of a cloud, or the mirror of the sky in a pool; it is always the air—real air that you seem to breathe, that fascinates you, and gives life and reality to the canvas"—(Meyer). M. Ménard tells us that Dupré had his own peculiar method of painting, *finishing* his pictures with the sky.

There is no published record of incidents of his biography during the later period of his life. He retired during the Franco-German war to a very singular fishing village on the shore of the channel—Cayeux, near Abbéville, where he found excellent material for the study of *sandy dunes*, for Cayeux is built absolutely on the sands, and, we are informed, there is not another village resembling it in France; it is a "pile of houses" of mud and straw, built with no regard to arrangement, at unequal heights on the shore, and the sand fills the streets knee-deep when the west wind blows. In this curious retreat Dupré lived for some time in absolute retirement, and migrated afterwards to Barbizon, where he died on the 7th of October, 1889.

The best lithographs of Dupré's works are those of Français and Mouilleron. Louis Marvy, who died in 1850, has made excellent engravings of Dupré's earlier works. He was a pupil of Dupré, and has engraved also from Décamps, Cabat, Diaz, and others. He also painted some remarkable landscapes, engravings of which are published in a work compiled for the purpose—"*Un Été en Voyage*."

THE SETTING SUN. BY DUPRÉ.

In the year 1831 M. Lenormant selected a "bataillon" of "coming men," coupling together Aligny and Corot; Delaberge and Rousseau; Cabat and Jules Dupré; including in his eulogium also Giroux, Regnier, Gué, Jolivet and Paul Huet; and in 1882 Dupré and Cabat were the only veterans of all the "bataillon" who survived to rejoice in the triumph of the principles in art that they had fought for, and to a great extent initiated.

Our sketch of the biography of Dupré is more unsatisfactory and incomplete than any of the others that we have attempted, but the comparative meagreness of it must not be made, in any degree, a measure of its importance. Dupré differed from the others in many respects. He was not a disciple of Fourrier; he was in no degree involved in the hatching of political theories; he never posed to any public as a public man; he loved a family life, not a phalanstère; he never (to use an expressive phrase), "played for the gallery"; and, as a consequence, the details of the story of his life were not put upon record by his contemporaries. This is a distinct loss to us.; an account of his life and work in England, for example, in the years 1835 to 1839 would be interesting; a record of his early intimacy with Cabat, of his point of view of his affection for Rousseau, and of Rousseau's quarrel with him, still more so; and, from a critic's point of view, his own comparative estimate of his own powers early in life, and later. It would be interesting, also, to have his own apology for his retirement during the war to Cayeux; why were *none* of these Barbizon painters in the ranks, or in Paris? Many

feuilletonists have invented, at a late date, anecdotes and
narratives about Dupré, with which it would have been
pleasant to enlarge our biography, if it were not that, on
examination, they appeared inconsistent, fanciful, untrust-
worthy, or obviously untrue.

CONCLUSION.

A Retrospect of French Landscape Art [during the Present Century, in its Connection with the Secular Development of Painting in General.

———•———

A SHORT chapter of notes* of the course of events that led up to the Barbizon School of landscape, may be useful to those who wish to study more closely the details of this interesting episode in art.

The history of the development of modern French painting and of its stages of classicism, romanticism, classic-romanticism, idealism, orientalism, naturalism, impressionism, realism, and so forth, is made the subject of fanciful theories by various writers ; there is no doubt about its being closely inter-woven with the political and social incidents of the time. The Revolution and the Terror produced both David and Géricault, whose early childhood passed in those years (from 1791 onwards) of which a contemporary historian has said that he " never remembered then to have seen the sun shine." And Géricault preserved, from his birth and from the times that followed it, a similar impression, of which his painting is the gloomy mirror. He never painted woman, nor child, nor sunshine.

The war fever of Napoleon's career, and especially the

* Taken principally from the work of Herr Meyer.

plunder in pictures that he brought home, which Géricault was assiduous in studying, and wrote, "Never before—never in Athens nor in Rome—have the citizens had greater facilities for the study of the arts and sciences than France now gives in her schools"; the uneasy dog-sleep, or swoon of exhaustion, under the Bourbon restoration, broken by the short and sharp July revolution; Louis Philippe's citizen reign, and the underground volcano of communism that corroded it; the nursery garden of polite culture that flourished in the restful reign of Louis Napoleon, the increased commerce with other nations at peace, and a hundred similar social and political incidents, have had their influence on art.

The overlapping stages of the development do not admit of chronological arrangement.   They are not clearly contemporary with any accessory causes, they follow political events, or seem to predict their imminence and the presence of the forces producing them.

They are reflected in contemporary literature, in the drama, and in social life.   No feature of Herr Meyer's great work on the subject is more interesting than the skill and precise criticism with which he pairs off, in each period or phase of his art history, the painters and the writers together.

Landscape painting throughout followed closely the phases and transitions of all other branches of art, but no other branch has developed so rapidly, or to such perfection, as landscape painting has.   The new revelation that has come to the painters of landscape is harder to define in language than to appreciate in its result.   They have learned that their appreciation of scenery must have two distinct motives—the one to discover in it a finished and perfect *ensemble*, a *totum teres atque rotundum*, so that every landscape is to them a beautiful and individual object for the sense of sight to apprehend as a whole; and the other motive is to seek and to find, in the life of the light and the atmosphere, a world of undefined and indefinable sympathies with the emotions of man; to raise painting, in this relation, to a level with musical art.

This revelation is not altogether a new thing. In part it is a revival of principles known to the seventeenth century, to the precursors and pupils of Rembrandt, to Watteau, and to others. But the painters of the modern revival of landscape arrived at them independently, by sympathy with the general romantic development in all branches of art, and they have carried them very far in the skill with which they can seize and place on record a fugitive phase of scenery, and bring it into sympathy with their own mood or emotion, as music has, at all times, boasted of doing; and fanciful as this sounds, those who do it claim above all other titles that of realist, faithful portrayers of the things they really see, and they select their subjects from the most commonplace realities of scenery. "The nearest field, the fringe of a scanty wood, a tangle of bushes on a heath, a trampled village road, a marsh in a flat meadow, have the same claims to be depicted with secular forests, bold peaks of the Alps, or the luxuriant grandeur of the boldly-accidented formations of the landscapes of the South. For the same creative forces of Nature are displayed in all; and everywhere to the painter's eye her soul ascends in the transfiguring glamour of the air and light."

The landscape of Poussin and Claude knows nothing of this poetry of the light and the circumambient air; nor did they copy any work of Nature as a whole, but constructed their scenery—their world of "*Götterbergen, Götterbäumen, Götterlüften*" (as Vischer calls it)—the stage for their figures to appear on—piecemeal from local studies made here and there.

The landscape of the eighteenth century—of Boucher, Pater,

and Lancret—differed from theirs only in that it was not heroic but Arcadian, with foliage delicately fluttering over the shepherds and shepherdesses in velvets and silks, and underfoot a lawn like a carpet. Watteau alone saw something of the truth of the poetry of landscape, and celebrated all alone the wonders of the play of light. In the latter half of the century came a few French landscape painters in closer sympathy with Nature. Joseph Vernet, poor Lantara of Fontainebleau,* Bruandet, a close student of Ruysdael, and Hubert Robert, a lover of ruins; *rari nantes* among a multitude of miniaturists who located their splendidly-dressed clients in appropriate Arcadian gardens.

But all this was killed at a blow, with all else that was graceful and pretty, by the paralysis of the Revolution of 1789, and the spectre of David and the antique stalked abroad. We are not interested in David himself; the Elysian *entourage* of the Olympian life of his gods and heroes has nothing to do with landscape. HENRI VALENCIENNES † was, in landscape, the leader and advocate of his school. His work on perspective and landscape‡ became the text-book of the classical school. He warmly enjoined his pupils to perfect themselves in ideal landscape by the study of Homer, Virgil, Theocritus, and Longinus. His principal pupils were Jean Victor Bertin § and Xavier Bidauld,‖ who, although Bertin showed talent for composition, and Bidauld was an industrious and conscientious student of nature, achieved no excellence. "They were chained," Herr Meyer says, "to the dead tradition," and one

* See page 14 of the Introduction to "Millet."
† 1750—1819.
‡ *Elements de perspective pratique, suivis de réflexions sur le paysage.*
§ 1775—1842. (See Biography of Corot.)
‖ 1758—1846.

description of their pictures will suffice for the whole of their monotonous school. "There was always a gracefully modulated rising ground, sometimes on the right, sometimes on the left side of the picture, and over against it, on the other side, a plain and some groups of noble trees whose foliage was mathematically symmetrical. In the middle ground there was a river, and on the banks magnificent buildings, temples, palaces, Italian houses with grandiose and massive walls; or, the other way about, the vegetation was on the second plan, and the architectural glory in the foreground; finally, in the distance there was the inevitable classic chain of hills. A rock, a hill, foliage, a stream, a ruin, they were always the same 'pledges in pawn,' which the painter varied nothing but the position of, giving out every new combination for a new landscape. That Nature is an organism whose limbs are in sympathetic living relation with the whole, and so vary in appearance as the whole varies; they had no suspicion of that."

Such was the typical landscape of the classical school established by the canons of Valenciennes, of which may be mentioned Felix Boisselier, Bacler d'Albe, Dunouy, Louise Sarrazin de Belmont, Amédée Bourgeois, and Turpin de Crissé, and, if some among them made timid approaches towards a more natural style, none departed from the canons established for their guidance, principally for their restraint, by Valenciennes. Two painters, Didier Boguet and Pequignot, names little heard of, worked in Italy and deserve more attention than the others. Of Pequignot especially Delaborde says, that "in the few drawings and pictures he has left he shows a mixture of poetry inspired by Nature, and of elegant invention." And at the end of the list comes the name of Achille Michallon, the master of Corot, a painstaking student of the two Poussins.

G

He died in 1822.* He was a painter who, had his life been prolonged, might have taken his place in the ranks of the men of 1830.

A few independent painters, besides those inspired by Italian skies, had, in the meantime, found touch with the landscape scenery and the skies of their northern homes, and without refractory opposition to the maxims of Valenciennes, painted homelier and truer landscape than their orthodox companions. Of these Louis Demarne† gave subjects of French village life, something in the manner of Berchem, men and animals straying peacefully to and fro in a homely landscape; and Louis Etienne Watelet,‡ whom Herr Meyer characterizes as:" the only landscape painter of his period who was consistently independent of Valenciennes. He lived a long life and was a prolific worker for more than half a century, producing a most varied series of landscapes, inclining now to the old and then to the new, all his life long, and striving to combine the irreconcileable." His liberation from " the academical swaddling clothes" (as Herr Meyer expresses himself) dates from the Salon of 1824, and his pictures of the *Lake of Nemi* and the *Cascades of Tivoli* exhibited then. He sought romantic effect in the choice of his subjects, "lonely Alpine valleys with birling mountain torrents, gloomy forests, and pine-clad rocks in a storm, in which a study of real nature is mingled with recollections of Ruysdael and Everdingen; or a village in Normandy in a shower of summer rain, . . . but all his pictures," Herr Meyer adds, "are hopelessly alike, and of that 'petrified movement' that catches only the surface show, but not the life of the landscape."

* The epoch-making Salon in which Géricault and Ingres made their debût was 1819.   † 1754—1829.   ‡ 1780—1864.

Two other painters, Michel Grobon and André Jolivard, have the same deficiency of apprehension that Watelet betrays. They can neither of them be classed as painters of the romantic school, although they were a decided advance upon that of Valenciennes.

We have dealt only with the Landscape hitherto. In other branches David was supreme, with the single exception of PRUD'HON. It was in the height of David's popularity that Prud'hon appeared; returning from Italy deeply impressed with his studies of the masters of the Cinquecento, especially Leonardo, and of Correggio. David recognised his talent, but called him "the Boucher of his period," and said that he pursued form and expression in a groove that was always the same. But his pictures show spontaneity of feeling, an unaffected delight in picturesque beauty, and a lively, imaginative faculty that all unconsciously merges the sensual in the Ideal. He never departs from nature; form and action he catches from nature most happily, by close observation, but always from the point of view that is natural to him. His especial characteristic is a fresh, outspoken sense of the outward appearance, which makes no pretension to any depth of meaning, but sets its whole heart upon the playful enjoyment of existence and goes on its way rejoicing in the sunny light of day.

He was patronised by Napoleon, and much neglected in consequence by the Bourbons after the Restoration. He died in 1823. He stands in the history alone and unlinked with either his contemporaries or his successors. He was the only great painter of his period who made successful revolt from the principles of David, but he had no pupils ready to carry on his work after his death—the Romantic school, starting from Géricault, was independent of him—but many of the traits of the later romantic and realistic schools reflect his principles. It was peculiar to him that his art was absolutely unaffected by the character of his period.

The ROMANTIC school of painting was founded by GÉRICAULT, in 1819. He was born in 1790, and studied first under Carl Vernet, whom he left, saying that "under the pretence of horses he had been set to draw *hares*"; afterwards, under Guérin, in company with Delacroix, Scheffer, Cogniet, and Champmartin. And there, says M. Chesneau, "he persisted in infusing life into the dead studies that Guérin gave him to copy, and Guérin gave him up."

But it was in the Louvre that he studied most insatiably, copying all sorts of masters of all sorts of schools, and, as M. Chesneau says, "under his enterprising brush, Dutch masters, Michelangelos and Correggios, were turned into *Gericaults.*"

He electrified the public in 1812 with a life-size and life-like portrait of a mounted *Chasseur of the Imperial Guards* (M. Dieudonné), "a calm cavalier on a furious horse"; and again in 1814, with a *Wounded Cuirassier*, personifying, with a pathos unknown to David, French heroism, and the well-remembered then recent misery of the Russian retreat.

In 1817 he went to Italy, visited Rome and Florence, and copied and studied especially the works of Caravaggio, Titian, Raphael, Rembrandt, Rubens, Prud'hon, and other masters, and in 1819, after this course of study, sprang upon the bewildered disciples of David his *Raft of the Medusa*—which marks the epoch of the beginning of the transition of French art to the new realism, and was the starting-point of the Romantic school.

"Without foreknowledge of the extreme development that his reform was destined to assume, and before he had even made it secure, but all the glory of this triumph belongs not the less to him," says M. Chesneau.

EUGÈNE DELACROIX was his immediate heir, and in 1822, with a picture entitled, *Dante and Virgil, conducted by Plegias, cross the lake which surrounds the infernal city of Dité*, initiated the long series of representations of moral and physical torture, shipwrecks, executions and massacres, which are the characteristic subjects of this gloomy school—in harmony with the literature of its day, when the "Poetry of Despair," as Goethe calls it, was in fashion; on the Stage portrayed with energetic realism by Frédéric Lemâitre, and, in Poetry, by Alfred de Musset, analyst of "all vices, all misery, all crimes, in ever madder and madder combinations, and outbursts ever more and more frantic," and by Victor Hugo, who says in his preface to *Les Orientales*, 1829, that "he directs his art to stirring the soul to its depths by means of the horrible and the dreadful, which he sought to realise by minute delineation of accessories to illusion, by richness of colour, and picturesque accuracy of detail in the *outside husk* of real life."

So painting and literature selected the same accessories; strange and uncouth individuals selected from a stirring time in modern history, endowed with unbridled sensitive impulses and passions, and placed in rare and perilous situations; a restless change of mood; contrasts of the ridiculous and the horrible; a blood-curdling climax to the story—and all that in the colour, dress, and locality of the past, in luxuriant scenery revived from chronicles, antiquarian research, and old pictures, transporting the imagination back to ancient times. Such pictures were well calculated to shatter the nerves of the people of the day eager for excitement.

Side by side with Géricault and the Romantic school, INGRES and the IDEALISTS were attacking the classical phalanx with fascinating studies from the nude, not classically chaste and cold and statuesque, but representations of living and palpitating humanity, influenced by study not of the antique but of Italian art, and not, like the Romantic nude, representative of agony, passion, or death, but of a sweet and placid *ideal* of perfection in repose. The painters of this school, by virtue of their reference to the Ideal, were classed as classic-romanticists. Herr Meyer's résumé on the subject is interesting.

"So the ROMANTIC tendency ruled, nearly absolute, the Art of the Restoration; and, whilst it took modern painting by storm, it drove the classical school off the field, thereby declaring simultaneous war with the art tradition, and the ideal form world. The new art could find no room for the latter, its frame was full; with Nature, on the one hand, caught as she showed and shone at a given moment; with the free portrayal, on the other, of the passing pictures of individual fancy, which, again, clothed themselves in tangible robes of reality. The whole world of things in their changeful showing and glowing, in the flitting movement of their ever-changing existence; the world as the modern mind (like the stormy surface of the sea) reflects it in a thousand broken waves, was made the subject of pictorial representation. And so the crude barrier of the line, of the Form that contains all quiet and safe within its compass, was broken through, as the picture of a life raised above the need and the strife of accident had cast it, like an unreal shadow, away.

"But the Ugly came into Art with the Undefined. All outlines, all forms shook and swayed in the concealing and revealing play of the light. In the reciprocal colour play of all visible objects, the Shape trembled and melted away; lost its independent significance; was snatched from the repose of its harmonious perfection by the hurry and antagonisms of reality;

was overwhelmed also by the stormy passion of the drama, and torn from its place by the 'throw' of picturesque movement which the new tendency gave to it.

"But French art (and here we see the comprehensiveness— the simultaneous apprehension of antagonistic ideas that is characteristic of modern thought) was not contented with this development of the Picturesque. Side by side with this tendency another came to the front, which restored Form, properly so called, to its rightful position—the '*stylvolle Bildung*' of the human body (that is to say, its representation with all the grandeur and grace of the antique) which shows us the life of it, as it were, transfigured, and a soul superior to all straits and troubles is poured into its containing body, and fills it, like a vessel, full of peace to the brim. The formal element, the Line and the Drawing (which had remained strongly marked in Géricault, but was neglected by his followers), was, in an independent way, taken up again, and made the basis of a method in art peculiar to INGRES and his school, and a few assimilating men of talent.

"Their aim, in which they differ from Géricault and the Romantics proper, is to portray a figure perfect in itself, and conveying an ideal significance. Hence follow their antagonisms to the Romantic school ;—they take up tradition again, and connect themselves with bygone periods in art,— they revive (in another manner, it is true) the obsolete standards of the preceding classical period,— they bring the Antique, as well as the Christian myth, back again into art, not in the guise of modern life as the Romantics did, but in its own proper character,—finally, they form a close community, a group, with one common purpose and one method, gathered round one eminent man who is the Master of their School."

The above seems to set out very clearly the antagonism of

the Romantics, and the Classic-Romanticists or Idealists, as they are indifferently called—Ingres and Géricault.

They came in simultaneously with the Bourbons. Ingres, returning from Rome, exhibited his first Salon picture (which was the gage of battle with his own personal masters and disappointed friends the Classic* school, as well as with Géricault) in 1819, in the same room with the *Raft of the Medusa;* but it was not before 1830 that the Idealists found themselves in harmony with the sentiment, the reactionary retrospect of the passing period, and a time came at last when Georges Sand wrote : " What can it signify to Ingres the possession of wealth and fame ? For him there is only one verdict in the world, that of Raphael, whose ghost looks over his shoulder."

The Bourbon reign was an episode of incessant stubborn strife between the agencies of progress, political and æsthetic, and the reactionary Monarchical idea—to the former Géricault, to the latter Ingres was congenial. The July Revolution, the accession of the Citizen king, the glorification of the burgher class, and the temporary triumph of reactionary principles in art, were all signs of a time of weariness with strife, of a reconciliation, a quiet *modus vivendi,* under favour of which the nation, as a whole, took breathing time, and was rather engaged taking stock of its past than in seeking out new paths. It is obvious that this prevailing mood was in the highest degree unfavourable to, and suspicious of, the group of landscape painters, championed by the communist Thoré, who made their début at the crisis. On the contrary, the doctrines of Ingres, eclectic of the truth in the old and the new, animating the classic and idealising the romantic, showed the citizen world

* Everybody expected in Ingres a. champion of the doctrines of his master, David, in his early allegiance to which he had won the Prix de Rome.

that sober *via media* that men of business and common-sense prefer. Had the "Men of 1830" been the men of 1848, their success would have been immediate and secure.

In the expression "a School of Art" is generally implied a group of artists formed in the doctrines of a master, who is the founder of their school. This can be predicated of Ingres and his followers, but *not* of the Romantics, for the romantic point of view left each individual painter free to follow the bent of his own subjective—imaginative—faculty; and bound him to no law, and to no limitation but such as he found within himself. His task was to be only on the one hand the practical, effectual utterance of the emotions that he really experienced; and, on the other, to give to his picture the captivating truth of reality, to watch and wait for the most trivial and accidental phenomena of nature, and to perpetuate the passing moment in which they suddenly appear and are lost again.

Romanticism, in this double aim, is therefore on the one hand realistic, and on the other hand fantastic; and each painter, according to his natural disposition, inclines to the one or the other extremity of the scale. Géricault, for example, and ARY SCHEFFER represent the two poles of Romanticism. In the middle between them is Delacroix, and it is characteristic that he was the colourist who dissipated all outline and fixity of term in his effects of colour, and at the same time strove for the expression of the most fearful intensities of emotion in humanity; whilst, in the work of DÉCAMPS, the element of colour, the purely picturesque view of things, attained a perfectly independent (untaught) development.

The work of Décamps, its independence of all teachers, its variety, especially its wonderful perfection in the treatment of light and shadow, is one of the most remarkable and important products of the period.* Of the Barbizon school, Diaz especially learned much from the example of Décamps.

Ary Scheffer's peculiar genius in the expression of the more tranquil, subdued emotions was a healthy admixture in the romantic feast of horrors of the time, and was in harmony with the peaceful poetry of Lamartine. He was Dutch by extraction, but educated entirely in France, a recalcitrant pupil of Guérin; and the character of his work is allied with the contemporary painting of Germany.

The contrast is remarkable between him and Décamps, in whom the Romantic principle that, to the eye of the painter, the commonest objects of every-day life and the highest subjects of the poet's verse are alike and equal in their relation to the picturesque, culminates.

In respect of its dazzling effects of light and colour, the work of Décamps is compared unfavourably with the quieter simplicity of the Dutch masters; of Pieter de Hooch and of Nicolaas Maes, and most notably of Rembrandt, to a kinship with whom Décamps nevertheless has a claim. As a colourist he is surpassed by Bonington, who rivals him in the manage-

---

* Preoccupied with colour and light, Décamps selected for his subjects scenery parched by the sunshine or tossed about by the weather; crumbling earth, stagnant water, ruined buildings, and the poverty-stricken lives of the lower classes, shepherds and beggars in tattered clothes. Such shabby, worn-out, and ragged objects absorb the light more deeply. "The brilliant and startling truthfulness with which the sunbeam is arrested upon old chalky, crisp, and weather-beaten walls, and set in contrast with the deep shadows, which hide all the objects in their recesses in darkness, out of which they seem to emerge into sight gradually, uncertain in shape and subdued in colour, and scarcely recognisable; and finally, in between the light and the shadows, the tender intermediary play of the chiaroscuro, in which the figures and objects float, as it were, dimly foreshadowed in a veil."

ment of light. Camille Roqueplan and Isabey are mentioned as followers of the methods of Bonington.

In the universal compromise of Louis Philippe's period, DELAROCHE, and historical painting, came forward as a mediator between the extravagance of the Romantic and the hyper-idealism of the reformed classical tendencies ; between the schools, that is to say, of Delacroix and Ingres.

He was far inferior to either of these masters in originality and in natural talent, but he attained to greater eminence than either in the estimation of his contemporaries. His paintings, as works of art and as illustrations of historical events, gave a clearly defined expression to the *sentiment of the age;* and satisfied at the same time *the æsthetic standard of the educated classes*—in substance and in form—in form (style), by the happy mean that he struck between the extremes of the two contending schools; in substance, by the choice of his subjects : great crises of history, in which the destiny of one eminent individual has been the climax of a course of events epoch-making in the history of the world. His precise epoch is the July Revolution, when the critical study of the personal *details* of history was already the popular, prevailing tendency of literature. The realm of poetry and fiction, he said, has been exhausted by the Old Masters, and, before them, that of the religious myth and legend ; and the study of the plastic beauty of the human body carried to its highest perfection. What was left, but to portray purely human events from a dramatic point of view, and in a form that should, above all else, be—not so much *exalted*, as—the indisputable counterpart of the reality ? He appreciated the great results that the Romantics had attained by the study of scenes of agony and strife, but he was also, like Ingres, penetrated with a sentiment of the dignity and the importance of plastic form—of the duty of giving it in the human body in its highest perfection, and while stamping it, unmistakably and in the first place, with its *real character*, of making it beautiful also.* His mission in the art world was to inculcate the excellence of sobriety and moderation in all tendencies. He had no peculiarity of style to transmit to his followers, no marked originality or definite rule of practice to bind them together ; but he founded a School—of which may be mentioned Gerôme, Hamon, Hebert, Gendron, Jalabert, Landelle, Antigna, Ed. Frère, Edmond Hédouin—*and he was the last man who did so*, before the new régime, which sets up, instead of masters and leaders of schools, the independent individual impulse of each new aspirant in art in the direction peculiar to his own disposition and genius.

LEOPOLD ROBERT is a peculiar and independent representative of a phase of art that marks a transition from historical painting to genre. He was a zealous pupil and always a worshipper of David : and it is noteworthy that he attributes even to David the use of the hackneyed and infinitely-abused precept, "that Nature was the only guide a man could follow without being led astray."

His first important works—romantic scenes of brigand life in Italy—combined a sufficient memory of the antique to do

* His work must be studied in three periods :—(1). Antecedent to his first Italian journey in 1834. Grounded upon the Flemish schools, especially the dignity, and "life-glow" of Van Dyck, and the descriptive, character-reading realism of Holbein and Dürer, not uninfluenced by the hard outline and simplicity of the Florentines. (2). After his return from Rome, and marriage with the daughter of Horace Vernet, his monumental and religious work, showing a strong leaning towards the ideal, also a great advance in "picturesque treatment, comprehension of the chiaroscuro, and of the combined result." (3). From the death of his wife, in 1845, the series of mournful pictures, no longer instinct with dramatic life and action, but expressive of patient suffering; encroaching upon the descriptive province of literature, and, like Ary Scheffer's similar work, failing their effect.

justice to the hereditary nobility of form and action characteristic of the Roman peasantry with a close adherence to
reality, and, at the same time, a vivid appreciation of the
romantic element and of the picturesque costumes, the vigour
of character and the passion and impulse of the people.

"Finally, his simplest pictures produced an effect, that was
quite peculiar to them, of silence and depth of feeling—a sensation of being in a solitude, shut out of the world—as if this
branch of the human family was the last remnant of a departed
beautiful world, and shut away in its own narrow circle, had
nothing whatever to do with the turmoil of the passions of the
period, but went in mourning for its own loneliness and for
the enmity of the tendencies of the age. This was nothing
but the mood of Robert's own life communicated to the figures
in his pictures; and this is their real charm, and their peculiar
art characteristic. He is, in this respect, almost the only
painter of modern times who is naive and unaffected in the
portrayal of real life, because his own heart beats in harmony
with the sentiment involved in his subject, and this intimate
sympathy of the man and the theme of his picture is an excuse
that glosses over many faults from which Robert was never
cured."

He subsequently painted a series of pictures of Italian peasant life,* and the criticisms that they evoked closely resemble
those written about the most "powerful" of the works of Millet,
whom he also resembled in personal character. The tragic

* His most important epoch-making picture (*The arrival of a party of
Roman harvest labourers in the Pontine Marshes*) was exhibited in the Salon
of 1831. There is a good engraving of it in *L'Artiste* of the year.
Vischer says: "The peasant leaning on the yoke between the pair of
powerful buffaloes—there is a Cincinnatus latent in the man; that noble
woman on the waggon, with the child in her arms—she might sit to
Raphael for a Madonna."

story of his hopeless passion for the Princess Charlotte Napoleon, and of his suicide, might be taken for a parody upon the "Sorrows of Werther."

It has not only a romantic interest in itself, but a direct bearing upon our subject also, because of the extreme to which Robert was the first to carry the expression of his own inner life in his pictures. "It is his own soul," Herr Meyer says, "that speaks out of all his works, and whatever he has achieved he always put his whole heart into the achievement of, with all his might, and with all the earnestness of his abundant nature. But the supplement to his '*geniality*,' and the quality to which he owes his important rank in modern art, is the broad, realistic drift of his genius, which is so closely mingled with that subjective element. He was a genuine artist. Therefore he discovered, even in everyday life, a beauty which before his time in its *immediate* reality had been unknown to painting."

Akin in tendency to Robert, but inferior in talent, were his friend Victor Schnetz, who was the Director of the French Academy at Rome in the years 1840—45 and 1853—58, and Bonnefond, both of David's school; and Rodolph Lehmann, Karl Müller, and Charles de Pignerolle, from that of Ingres; and Ernst Hébert, a pupil of Delaroche. Hebert is the most important name in this category. He achieved sudden eminence in 1851 by his celebrated picture, *The Malaria*, representing a Roman family on a punt, escaping down the Tiber to a healthier site. "Nothing but the picture itself can convey to the reader's mind the impressive melancholy effect that it produces on the mind. An uncanny (*unheimlich*) greyish blue tone is spread over the scene; a heavy, fever-pregnant atmosphere clings about the unfertile shore and the sluggishly creeping stream and the people already blighted by its baneful breath. There is a gloom about it that irresistibly grasps and clutches you tighter and tighter as you look at it, and the sensation is the more masterful over you because it is all produced by the pictorial effect of the picture, and has none of that obscure allusion to any poetical incident that is brought to bear on so many modern pictures. But the *tone* of the atmosphere, the mysterious light has penetrated all things alike with its foreboding element, absorbed all that is characteristic of the local colouring, and in the harmony of the general effect saturated the reality with the spirit of the scene. Moreover the landscape itself in its most subtle details has been closely studied and reproduced with a perfect truth of apprehension."

With the Revolution of 1848 came to the front a new phase of realism in art, which, however, was not a new discovery, but a revival, an advance upon the work of such painters as the brothers Le Nain in the seventeenth, and Jeanrat and Chardin in the eighteenth, centuries. It differed from the realism of Géricault, which sought for energy and emotion rather than the quiet, every-day appearance of nature; and it had no respect for the dignity of the object, but was directed rather by preference to the lowest and most vulgar or degraded forms. This style arose naturally out of the revolutionary doctrines of 1848, and was represented in its extreme tendency by COURBET in his figure pictures, principally of subjects of the coarsest features of peasant life.

But in landscape Courbet excels, and especially in the portrayal of the simplest scenery; not, however, with any view to "impressionism," or the subtle *management* of light, but to reproduce faithfully the *true* tones and lights in the simplest possible style.

In the higher and more pathetic treatment of this branch of realistic painting of scenes of peasant life, such as were dealt

with in literature by Georges Sand and the poet Pierre
Dupont, two painters stand pre-eminent—Millet, and Jules-
Adolphe Breton, who came to the front in the fifties. Breton's
style differs from that of Millet, and is more directed to the
qualities that a classic painter would esteem; but his subjects
of rustic life tell equally of the sufferings and of the *dignity* of
labour, and are treated in a natural and pathetic style, and
with exquisite feeling and skill.

The social life of the Second Empire was characterised by
the display of superficial culture and refinement—inwardly
corrupt, unprincipled. In conduct, in literature, and in art
alike, old standards were cast aside and individual licence pre-
vailed. The representative tendencies had no ideal at all,
classical, historical, religious, or æsthetic. Every man lived,
wrote, or painted, as it were, from hand to mouth, in his own
fashion, and all found sympathy somewhere—but the prevailing pleasures of the period, in comparison with which all
loftier aspirations were insignificant, were the pursuit of
wealth, and its expenditure in vice, in ostentation, and in
judicious bribery of the dangerous element of society—the
proletariat.

These three motives brought representative painters to the
front in three tendencies : *the abuse of the nude,* led by Couture,
Paul Baudry, and a very long list, of whom, however, there are
many more honourable than others, by whom the idealism—
the higher aim—of Ingres is perpetuated ; *the pursuit of Colour
for its own sake,* promoted by Décamps and the Orientalists,
culminating perhaps in our Barbizon DIAZ; finally, the study
of *the pathos of peasant life,* and of pastoral landscape, of which
Breton and MILLET, and, in their different lower style, the
imitators of Courbet are representative. At the same time,
an immense catalogue of painters of genre, illustrative of

details of social life of all periods, was numerically preponderant over all others; of whom among the more eminent in *historical* genre, are mentioned Comte, Hamman, Caraud, Hillemacher, Leman, finally MEISSONIER; in more *ancient* or quasi-classical subjects Gérôme excelled; in scenes of *modern life*, for the most part comical or pornographic, hundreds of every shade of merit and audacity competed to pander to the luxury of the age, and the most realistic and typical *Orientalist* is Fromentin, in respect of the accuracy of his study of the light and landscape, as well as of the social phenomena of the sunlit, picturesque eastern world.

But in combination with all other motives, and modified by all varieties of defects or points of excellence, the distinguishing characteristic of the painters of this period of art is stated in the one epithet—Realism.

All the changes and developments that we have attempted in this short abstract to indicate have been fully participated in by landscape art.

The works of the Romantic school of painters called attention home from the classical southern skies to those of France, and revealed the store of picturesque material to be found in the light of the northern day.

The first painter to give effect to this new revelation was Richard Parkes Bonington.* He exhibited in the Salon of 1822 two water-colour views of Normandy, "the freshness and fine 'colour-mood' (*Farbenstimmung*) of which gave the keynote to the new ideas about landscape that were stirring the younger members of the world of art."

* 1801—1828.

In 1824 these were followed by his marine pieces, full of light and feeling—"Only a flat sandy shore with a hut upon it, and fishermen's children at play, and in front the glassy expanse of the sea; but the sun is just plunging behind a heavy cloud, and radiates and reflects its parting gleams upon the glistening surface of the water. The whole scene is swimming in the light, and the poetical influence pours down with it on the plain and unpretending chalky coast. Common, every-day reality, ennobled by the painter's eye, which brings to the light of day its beauties hidden to a grosser apprehension—that is precisely what the Romantics wanted!"

Bonington was in harmony with them also in his predilection for mediæval scenes—for the crooked streets of Flemish and North Italy towns, weather-beaten houses, palaces and churches in their charm of colour mellowed by the exposure of centuries. "Dark dreams and memories of old times seem to haunt these ancient walls and towers, and to speak to us out of their ruddy golden tones that the air has given them in the course of ages. The atmosphere, at the same time, has broken up the architectural severity of the outline, and endowed the practical sobriety of the work of man with the freedom of the picturesque." His Venetian pictures are especially remarkable: there he had everything that he required, the incessant shimmer of water, the uninhabited palaces that were mirrored in it "like the submerged splendour of a fairy world."

Next after Bonington we must place John Constable, whose influence on the French school began with the Salon of 1824, where he exhibited several pictures which excited the admiration of the Romantic innovators, and among them of Delacroix. All the tendency of French Romanticism was in harmony with the work of these two masters, and the new views of landscape were developed rapidly. Eugène Isabey, the marine painter, and Camille Roqueplan,* a convert from the classical school, were among the first to follow the new principles. The speciality of Roqueplan was Dutch windmills and Dutch skies, and the valuation of light and air. They are followed by a numerous group, by Paul Huet, Charles de Laberge, and Camille Flers; finally by Louis Cabat and Dupré, Rousseau and Diaz—the Barbizon school.

"The landscape painter of the present generation is liberated from all tradition, and his object is truth—not only truth of local character in different latitudes and tracts of country, but truth in apprehension of the swiftly evanescent phenomena of natural life, of the effect of their combinations upon a trained and intelligent eye. For the painter has acquired a new power of seeing the picturesque element in nature flooded by light, and of understanding and seizing her secret in the instant of its revelation in the glamour of the circumambient day. And, at the same time, he has learned to penetrate deeply into the *mood-life* of nature. He discovers, in her atmospheric life, in her element-flooded brilliance, a harmony with the sentiments of the human heart, which comes to him not as a note from the external world, but as the revelation of an intimate affinity."

"And, in this way, modern landscape attains two things that earlier periods have only approached towards with difficulty: truth of appearance, and a profounder expression of feeling, by a profounder harmony with the *mood* of landscape. . . . . On the other hand, it has abandoned that luxuriance of picturesque accessories, that manifold variety of soils, vegetation, and formations of land and water which distinguish the methods of the earlier masters, including the Dutch.

* 1800—1855.

"In a word, the pervading characteristic of modern French landscape is realism. Commonplace nature, the first section at hand, the nearest field, the fringe of a scanty wood, the tangled bush on a heath, the well-trodden village street, the marsh in a flat meadowland—all that has the same right of presentation as the centenarian forests, the bold peaks of the Alps, the luxuriant grandeur and the accidented formation of the south. The same creative forces of nature are visible in all, and everywhere, to the painter's eye, her soul goes forth in the transfiguring gleaming of air and light. . . . .

"This landscape is therefore in its realism essentially picturesque, and brings forth out of nature the world of light, and tone, and moodful colour, and leaves the world of form disregarded. The genuine and pure picturesque effect, under equal and indifferent value of objects, is therefore the goal to which the ultimate phase of modern landscape is directed."

"And so modern painting has rung the changes of all possible kinds of subject, myth and fact, poetry and thought, the past and the present; and in the different decades has assumed all variations of method of form and colour. The age lives fast, and has carried art with it in its course. What is the ultimate stage of French painting to be ? In the latest phase of its development it has indisputably brought to some perfection the painting of scenes of peasant and pastoral life, and of landscape. . . . And in the best of this kind of work the face of nature is brought into harmony and sympathy with the painter's sentiment; the reality appears in its true colours, and at the same time gives utterance to the innermost mind of the man. What if here the first note has been found of that harmony between man and the universe which the present age is tending to realise more deeply and more earnestly than any former age ? If this landscape, which seems to be the last echo of a silenced epoch of art, should be the first fore-runner of the approaching reconciliation ; the first assurance that man is now about to find, in Reality, his eternal home, his Heaven, and his gods ? Landscape has hitherto followed after the periods of painting. What if it is called upon in our time to initiate a new era ? It is not impossible. The Present begins, in every way, so differently to the Past. The modern world has but little more to do with the material expression of the transcendental idea ; and modern art desires to be no more than the reflex of reality refined in the happy appreciation of it by the intellect. In this sense THE MODERN is infinitely in the right, quite as much as the Classical or the Romantic were. But if, in France, landscape is indeed to be the first small beginning, it must be followed, as a new subject for art, by the ennobled reality of human life ; and existing circumstances, political and social, afford small hope for this."*

* The above was written in 1867.

.

APPENDIX.

(Compiled by E.G.C.)

In the companion volume on "Millet, Rousseau, and Diaz," will be found in the Appendix a list of "Some of the Principal Private Collections containing examples of the Barbizon School."

The following Lists have been made as complete as possible, but, owing to the fact that works of art in private collections sometimes change hands with comparative frequency, it is impossible to make anything like complete lists of pictures by the artists. Any additions or corrections for a future edition will be gratefully received by the Editor of the series—"Biographies of the Great Artists," care of Messrs. Sampson Low, Marston & Co., St. Dunstan's House, Fetter Lane, London.

COROT.

I. BIBLIOGRAPHY.*

Burty (P.), "Exposition de l'Œuvre de Corot. Notice Biographique" (Paris, 1875).

Clarétie (J.) Corot ("Peintres et Sculpteurs Contemporains, I. 5"), 1884.

Dumesnil (H.), Corot—"Souvenirs intimes" (portrait à l'eau forte).

Montrosier (Eugène). Corot ("Les Artistes Modernes").

Robaut (A.), Corot ("Galerie Contemporaine").

Robaut, "L'Œuvre de Corot" (in progress).

Rousseau (J.), Corot, suivi d'un Appendice par A. Robaut ("Bibliothéque d'Art Moderne.")

Silvestre, "Histoire des Artistes vivants," 1856. Pt. 3, Corot.

"Art Journal." July, 1889, by R. A. M. Stevenson (London).

"Art and Letters," 1882, II., Pts. 4 and 5 (London).

"Athenæum," February 27th, 1875 (London).

"L'Art" (1875). Vol. I., pp. 241, and 269, by Jean Rousseau, II. 384, and III. 23 and 47 (*vente* Corot); II. 109, 157, 257; "Exposition des Œuvres de Corot," by E. Delephard; 1879, Vol. XIX., p. 224, by A. Robaut; 1882, XXXI., p. 45, by A. Robaut (Paris).

"Century Magazine." June, 1889, by Mrs. Schuyler van Renssalaer.

"Contemporary Review." XXVI., p. 157 (London).

* See also the General Bibliography of the Barbizon School in the volume on "Millet, Rousseau, and Diaz."

"Gazette des Beaux-Arts."   1861, XI., 416, by P. Mantz ; 1873, n.s.
     VII., p. 330, Laurent-Richard Coll., by R. Ménard ; 1875, n.s. XI.,
     p. 330, by J. Buisson (Paris).
" Magazine of Art," 1888, pp. 181 and foll., by D. C. Thomson.
" Overland Monthly." XV., p. 468.
" Portfolio." Vol. I. (1870), p. 60. Vol. VI. (1875), p. 146, by René
     Ménard (London).
" Revue des Musées," Octobre, 1889 (3me année, No. 49) (Paris).

II. Some of the Principal Pictures Painted By Corot.

At Break of Day, *H. C. Gibson, Esq., Philadelphia.*
Banks of a River, *Mrs. Borie, Philadelphia.*
Banks of the Stream, *M. Maurice Gentien, Paris.*
Baptism of Christ, *Church of St. Nicholas de Chardonnet.*
Bent Tree, The (trees with man in boat in foreground ; distant lake ; grey
     morning), *A. Young, Esq., Blackheath.*
Biblis (Corot's last work) [Salon, 1875, Secrétan Coll., and Paris
     Exhibition, 1889], *M. Otlet, Brussels.*
Birch Trees [Dreyfus Coll., Paris].
Birch Trees, The, *M. A. Batta.*
Bridge at Mantes [Faure and Defoer Colls.].
Broken Tree (evening effect through trees, with fallen tree in foreground ;
     cottages on the right), *A. Young, Esq., Blackheath.*
Brook, The, *M. de St. Albin, Paris.*
Brook of the Black Spring, Valley of the Loue (1855) [Laurent-
     Richard Coll.].
Château of Fontainebleau (etched) [Goldsmidt Coll.], *M. Fauré-Lepage,*
     Paris.
Christ in the Garden of the Mount of Olives (1849), *Langres Museum.*
Coliseum at Rome, *Louvre.*
Concert, The [J. Dupré Coll.], *Duc d' Aumale.*
Corot—Portrait of Himself (in a blouse and black velvet cap, with a
     palette in his hand), *Gallery of Portraits of Painters by themselves, Uffizi,*
     Florence.
Cottage, The (1871, etched) [Hoschedé Coll.].
Dance of Cupids (1866), *C. A. Dana, Esq., New York.*
Dance of Nymphs, *Jay Gould, Esq., New York.*
Dance of Nymphs, *J. S. Forbes, Esq., London.*
Dance of Nymphs, *Louvre.*

Dance of Nymphs. *T. G. Arthur, Esq., Glasgow.*
Dante and Virgil (1859), *bequeathed by Corot to the Louvre.*
Dante and Virgil, *Boston Museum, U.S.A.*
Daphnis and Chloë (1845).
Democritus and the Abderites (1841), *Mantes Museum.*
Destruction of Sodom (1844).
Diana surprised Bathing (1836).
Drinking-place, *M. F. Hertz, Paris.*
Drinking-place (cattle in a pool, luminous sky), *A. Young, Esq., Blackheath.*
Drunkenness of Silenus (1838), *M. Dollfus, Paris.*
Edge of the Forest—Morning [Laurent-Richard Coll.].
Entrance to the Village, *M. Detrimont.*
Evening (1839) [Laurent-Richard Coll.].
Evening. *Miss Cooper, New York.*
Evening, *Mme. Cottier, Paris.*
Evening in Arcadia—A Pastoral (etched). *J. S. Forbes, Esq., London.*
Evening in Normandy. *Hamilton Bruce, Esq., Edinburgh.*
Evening Star, *W. T. Walters, Esq., Baltimore.*
Farm at Toulon [Albert Spencer, Esq., New York].
Ferry Boat, The (etched), *Heer Mesdag, The Hague.*
Fisherman—Morning. *M. Roudillon, Paris.*
Fisherman, The Little, *M. G. Claudon, Paris.*
Fisherman's Wife, The, *M. Ernest May.*
Fishermen (1874) *Mme. C. Acloque, Paris.*
Flight into Egypt (1840), *Church at Rosny, near Mantes.*
Ford, The [Erwin-Davis, Esq., New York].
Ford, The [Duncan Coll.] (etched), *M. Henri Verer, Paris.*
Forest of Coubron—The Glade [Saulnier Coll., Paris].
Forest of Fontainebleau [Salon, 1846].
Frog Pond, *Mme. Cottier, Paris.*
Gathering Flowers [Faure Coll.].
Goatherds, *Le Comte Daupeas, Lisbon.*
Gust of Wind (sudden storm effect on bending trees), *A. Young, Esq.,*
   Blackheath.
Hagar in the Wilderness (1835), *bequeathed by Corot to the Louvre.*
Hagar in the Wilderness (1848), *Le Comte Doria, Ourroy.*
Hay-Cart, The, *J. S. Forbes, Esq., London.*
Heights of Ville d'Avray [Faure Coll.].
Homer and the Shepherds (1845), *Museum of Saint-Lo.*
In the Marshes [Morgan Coll.], *P. H. Sears, Esq., Boston, U.S.A.*

Italian Girl, *P. H. Sears, Esq., Boston, U.S.A.*
Lake of Garda [A. Wolff Coll.], *M. G. Lutz, Paris.*
Lake of Garda [Crabbe and Clappison Colls.], *J. S. Forbes, Esq., London.*
Lake of Nemi, *M. Hecht, Paris.*
Lake of Nemi (1865) [Morgan Coll.], *H. V. Newcomb, Esq., New York.*
Lake, The (etched) [Beriot and Brun Colls.].
Landscape with Figures, *M. Bellino, Paris.*
Landscape, with Nymphs Bathing (unfinished), *Boston Museum, U.S.A.*
Landscape with Rocks, *A. Sanderson, Esq., Edinburgh.*
Landscape, Diana's Bath, *Bordeaux Museum.*
Landscape, An Italian Scene (1848 ; retouched in 1855), *Douai Museum.*
Landscape, A Fête (presented by Corot), *Lille Museum.*
Landscape, *Lyons Museum.*
Landscapes (2), *La Rochelle Museum.*
Landscape, Morning, *Mme. Joliet, Paris.*
Landscape, *Montpellier Museum.*
Landscape (trees and lake ; woman with two cows on sandy road in fore-
    ground), *Hon. Mr. Justice Day.*
La Rochelle, *M. Ernest May.*
La Rochelle [Salon, 1852], *M. Robaut, Paris.*
Macbeth and the Three Witches (1859).
Mantes la Jolie (etched) (River with bridge ; distant view of town, and
    towers of the Cathedral), *A. Young, Esq., Blackheath.*
Mill, The—Landscape with figures [Saulnier Coll.].
Morning (1865) [Secrétan Coll.], *D. McIntyre, Esq., Montreal.*
Morning [Albert Spencer, Esq., New York].
Morning Effect, *M. Blancard.*
Morning Effect—Landscape, *Mme. Joliet, Paris.*
Nymphs and Fauns (Salon, 1869) [Laurent-Richard and Defoer Colls.].
Nymphs Dancing, *Cornelius Vanderbilt, Esq., New York.*
Nymphs of the Aube, *Mrs. Fell, Philadelphia.*
Nymphs playing with Cupid (1857), *M. le Dr. Charcot.*
Orchard, The, *General Hopkinson, London.*
Orchard, The, *presented by Corot to the town of Semur.*
Orpheus greeting the Morn, *D. Cottier, Esq., New York.*
Orpheus rescuing Eurydice (1861) [Saulnier Coll., Paris], *Heer Fop Smit,*
    Rotterdam.
Outskirts of Ville d'Avray [Dreyfus Coll.].
Pastoral—Souvenir of Italy (1873), *Dr. J. Forbes White, Dundee.*
Pond at Ville d'Avray, *M. Monjean.*

Pond, The, *M. P. Du Toict, Brussels.*
Pond, The, *M. P. Duché, Paris.*
Pond—Ville d'Avray (etched), *M. Georges Dutfoy.*
Ravine, A [Faure Coll.].
Ruin, The, *Hamilton Bruce, Esq., Edinburgh.*
Sand-pit, The, *M. Jules Ferry.*
Setting Sun, *J. D. Lankenau, Esq., Philadelphia.*
Shepherds' Star, The (1864), *Toulouse Museum.*
Sluice, The (etched), *M. Henri Vever, Paris.*
Solitude (etched), *J. S. Forbes, Esq., London.*
Solitude (1866), *Mme. de Cassin, Paris.*
Souvenir of Arleux-du-Nord (Salon, 1874), *M. Robaut, Paris.*
Souvenir of Italy [Laurent-Richard Coll.]
Souvenir of Limousin.
Souvenir of Marcoussis [Paris Exhibition, 1855. Purchased by the Emperor Napoleon III.].
Souvenir of Marissel, near Beauvais [Salon, 1867, Laurent-Richard Coll.], *M. Alfred Marme, of Tours.*
Souvenir of Mortefontaine (1864).
Souvenir of the Environs of Florence (1839), *Metz Museum.*
Souvenir of the Villa Pamphili (etched by Lalanne), *W. C. Quilter, Esq., M.P., London.*
St. Jerome, *presented by Corot to the Church at Ville d'Avray.*
St. Sebastian, Martyrdom of (1853), *T. W. Walters, Esq., Baltimore.*
Storm on the Sandhills [Constantine Ionides, Esq.]. *Now in America.*
Sunset, *J. D. Lankenau, Philadelphia.*
Toilet, The [Paris Exhibition, 1867], *M. V. Desfossés.*
Twilight [J. Dupré Coll.].
Twilight, *James Donald, Esq., Glasgow.*
View of Italy (1834).
View of the Beach at Biarritz (Exposition Corot, 1875), *Dr. Seymour, Paris.*
View of the Roman Forum, *Louvre.*
View of the Tyrol—Sunset (1850), *Marseilles Museum.*
View of Ville d'Avray, *Rouen Museum.*
Village of Marcoussis [Paris Exhibition, 1855: Defoer Coll.].
Ville d'Avray, *General Hopkinson, London.*
Ville d'Avray (1869) [etched], *Mrs. Hemenway, Boston, U.S.A.*
Ville d'Avray, *M. J. C. Roux, Marseilles.*
Wild Man of the Woods, *James Cowan, Esq., Glasgow.*
Willow Bank, *M. de Saint-Albin, Paris.*

Willows [Defoer Coll.].

Woman with the Tiger, *M. Clapisson, Paris.*

Wood and Lake (reproduced in Hamerton's "Landscape"), *Potter Palmer, Esq., Chicago.*

Wood-Cutters, *James Donald, Esq., Glasgow.*

Wood Gatherers (1874) [Morgan Coll.], *Corcoran Gallery of Art, Washington.*

Woods of Marcoussis [Erwin-Davis, Esq., New York].

III. MURAL PAINTINGS.

Corot was very fond of fresco painting, and practised it whenever he had the chance, chiefly in decorating the houses of friends. He, however, seldom did any work of this character for payment.

Six views of the neighbourhood of Ville d'Avray, on the walls of a kiosque in his garden there,—painted in 1849, on the occasion of his mother's birthday. They have now been transferred to canvas, and are the property of M. Alphonse Lemerre, the purchaser of Corot's house. They are :—

(1.) View of the Kiosque (upright).

(2.) Edge of the Wood, with a view of the Pond (upright).

(3.) Heights of Sèvres (oval).

(4.) Banks of the Pond, Ville d'Avray (oval).

(5.) Meadow with trees and cattle (oval).

(6.) Horses descending to the Drinking-place (oval).

"Views in Italy."—Painted on the walls of a bath-room in the house of M. Robert, at Nantes.

Panels in Décamps' house.

Panels in Daubigny's house at Auvers.

Four sacred subjects in the Church of Ville d'Avray :—

(1.) Adam and Eve driven out of Paradise.

(2.) The Magdalen in Prayer.

(3.) Baptism of Christ by St. John.

(4.) Christ in the Garden of Olives.

"Night." }
"Dawn." } Two decorative panels painted for Prince Demidoff.

IV. Paintings Exhibited by Corot at the Salon,
1827—1875.

1827. View at Narni: Campagna of Rome.
1831. View of Furia (Isle of Ischia) : Convent on the borders of the Adriatic.
1833. View in the Forest of Fontainebleau.
1834. A Forest: Sea-piece: Italian Scene.
1835. Hagar in the Desert: View at Riva (Italian Tyrol).
1836. Diana Surprised at the Bath: Campagna of Rome in winter.
1837. St. Jerome, landscape: View in the Isle of Ischia: Landscape—Sunset.
1838. Silence: View at Volterra (Tuscany).
1839. Italian Scene: Evening—landscape.
1840. Flight into Egypt, landscape: Sunset: A Monk.
1841. Democritus and the people of Abdera—landscape—taken from the Fables of Lafontaine: The Environs of Naples.
1842. Italian Scene, landscape—morning effect.
1843. Evening: Young Girls Bathing.
1844. Destruction of Sodom: Landscape with figures: Campagna of Rome.
1845. Homer and the Shepherds: Daphnis and Chloe: Landscape.
1846. Forest of Fontainebleau.
1847. Shepherd Playing with a Goat: Landscape.
1848. Italian Scene: Interior of a Wood: View of Ville d'Avray: Morning: Twilight: Evening: Morning Effect: Morning: Evening.
1849. Christ in the Garden of Olives: View at Volterra (Tuscany): View at Limousin: View at Ville d'Avray: Study in the Coliseum at Rome.
1850. Sunrise: Morning: Sunset (Italian Tyrol): Ville d'Avray.
1851. Sun Setting: Repose: Port of La Rochelle.
1853. Saint Sebastian: Morning: Evening.
1855. *(Universal Exhibition)* Morning: Marcoussis, near Montlhéry: Spring: Evening: Souvenir of Italy: Evening.
1857. Burning of Sodom: A Nymph Playing with a Cupid: The Concert: Setting Sun: Evening: Souvenir of Ville d'Avray: Morning (Ville d'Avray).
1859. Dante and Virgil, landscape: Macbeth, landscape: Idyl: Landscape with figures: Souvenir of Limousin: Italian Tyrol: Study at Ville d'Avray.

1861. Dance of Nymphs: Rising Sun: Orpheus: The Lake: Souvenir of Italy: Repose.
1863. Rising Sun: Study at Ville d'Avray: Study at Méry, near La Ferté-sous-Jouarre.
1864. Souvenir of Mortefontaine—Gust of wind.
1865. Morning: Souvenir of the Environs of Lake Nemi.
1866. Evening: Solitude: Souvenir of Vigen (Limousin).
1867. View of Mariselle near Beauvais—Gust of wind.
1868. Morning at Ville d'Avray: Evening.
1869. Souvenir of Ville d'Avray: "A Reader."
1870. Landscape with figures: Ville d'Avray.
1872. Souvenir of Ville d'Avray: Near Arras.
1873. Pastoral—The Shepherd.
1874. Souvenir d'Arleux du Nord: Evening: Moonlight.
1875. An antique dance: Woodcutter: Biblis.

V. ORIGINAL ETCHINGS BY COROT.*

1. Souvenir de Toscane.
2. Bateau sous les Saules—effet du Matin.
3. L'Etang de Ville d'Avray—effet du Soir.
4. Un Lac du Tyrol.
5. Souvenir d'Italie.
6. Environs de Rome.
7. Paysage d'Italie.
8. Campagne boisée.
9. Dans les Dunes.
10. Vénus coupe les ailes de l'Amour.
11. Vénus coupe les ailes de l'Amour (répetition de la planche précédente).
12. Souvenir des fortifications de Douai.
13. Le Dôme florentin.
14. Les Baigneuses.

LITHOGRAPHS.

1. La Garde meurt et ne se rend pas.
2. La Peste de Barcelone.
3. Une Fête de Village.

* Taken from Beraldi's "Les Graveurs du XIX. Siècle" (Paris, 1886), in which is given a full description of each plate and the different states.

4. Mdle. Rosalie—rôle de la mère Boisseau dans la Caisse d'Epargne, théâtre Comte.

AUTOGRAPHS.

"Douze Croquis et Dessins originaux, tracés sur papier autographique" (Avril—Mai, 1871), par Corot.

And three others :—1. "Sous bois-croquis" (1871). 2. "Le Fort détaché" (Arras, 1874). 3. "Lecture attachante" (1874).

Corot made as well some sixty-five drawings on bichromate glass, from which proofs were printed by photography—and about one thousand of his studies and pictures have been photographed by M. Arras and others. M. Georges Petit has published a series of six volumes, of twenty-five photographs in each, after paintings by him.

VI. ETCHINGS AFTER PICTURES BY COROT.

The English titles, by which they are best known in this country, are given.

The Lake	Etched by T. Chauvel.
The Ferry Boat	,, ,,
Ville d'Avray	,, ,,
The Pond (Ville d'Avray)	,, ,,
The Willow Bank	,, ,,
Solitude	,, ,,
The Setting Sun	,, ,,
Evening in Arcadia (a Pastoral)	,, Brunet-Debaines.
The Cottage	,, ,,
Storm on the Sandhills	,, ,,
The Heath	,, ,,
The Lake of Garda	,, L. Gautier.
The Canal (small)	,, ,,
The Cottage	,, ,,
The Heath	,, ,,
Sandcart	,, ,,
Nymphs and Fauns	,, W. Reid.
Mantes-la-Jolie	,, M. Lalanne.

Souvenir of Italy	Etched by M. Lalanne.
Dance of Nymphs (the picture in the Louvre) .	„ C. Kratké.
Landscape in the Tyrol	„ L. Desbrosses.
Goatherds	„ C. J. Beauverie.
The Lake of Garda	„ L. Leterrier.
In the Marshland	„ „
The Ferry	„ „
The Ford	„ G. M. Greux.
The Sluice (La Vanne)	„ Lopisgisch.
Evening (Le Soir) (small)	„ Felix Buhot.
The Chateau of Fontainebleau	„ Teyssonnières.

The above are the principal etchings after pictures by Corot ; besides these. however, various smaller etchings and lithographs by Bracquemond (7), Anastasie, Français, Lassalle, Laurens, Vernier, Brunet-Debaines, Chauvel, Marvey, Desavary, Henri Faure, Teyssonnières. G. Greux. &c., have appeared in the "Gazette des Beaux-Arts," "L'Art," "L'Artiste," "Cent Chefs d'Œuvre" (Paris, 1883), "Le Galerie Durand Ruel," "Le Musée Universel," and other publications, as well as in important sale catalogues, including those of MM. Hartmann, Laurent-Richard, Saulnier, Dreyfus, Faure, Oppenheim, &c., &c., and photogravures in those of MM. Defoer and Secrétan, as also in the publication. "Les Artistes Modernes" and Hamerton's "Landscape." In 1870 a collection of lithographs, with text by P. Burty, appeared in Paris under the title of "Douze Corot Lithographies, par Emile Vernier" (Lemercier & Cie.). Amongst those by Français we may mention, "Fauns," "Setting Sun," "Democritus."

DAUBIGNY.

VII. BIBLIOGRAPHY.*

Henriet (F.), "Charles Daubigny — Esquisse biographique" (Paris, 1857).

„   "Charles Daubigny et son Œuvre gravé" (Paris, 1875).

Clarétie (Jules), "Charles Daubigny" (Librairie des Bibliophiles).

* See also the General Bibliography of the Painters of Barbizon in the volume on "Millet, Rousseau, and Diaz."

" Daubigny et son Œuvre gravé, eauxfortes et bois," inédits par C. Daubigny, Karl Daubigny, et Léon Lhermitte (1875-78, Paris).
" Gazette des Beaux-Arts " (1874), n.s. IX., 254 and 464 (by F. Henriet).
" L'Art," XXV., p. 73 (1881), by F. Henriet.
" L'Artiste " (1857—6th series), I. 179, 195 ; (1878, n.s.) VIII. 400; IX. 51 (by Henriet).
" Magazine of Art," 1889, pp. 300 and 325, by D. C. Thomson.

VIII. SOME OF THE PRINCIPAL PAINTINGS BY DAUBIGNY.

Banks of a River, *M. J. C. Roux, Marseilles.*
Banks of the Cure, Morvan [Salon, 1864, and Paris Exhibition, 1889], *A. Young, Esq., Blackheath.*
Banks of a River (1859), *Mme. Joliet, Paris.*
Banks of the Loire [Defoer Coll.].
Banks of the Oise (Salon, 1859), *Bordeaux Museum.*
Banks of the Oise (Salon, 1861), *M. H. Vever, Paris.*
Banks of the Oise, *Mme. Veuce J. Rœderer, Havre.*
Banks of the Oise (1862), *M. Brullé, Paris.*
Banks of the Oise, *M. Vasnier, Rheims.*
Banks of the Oise, *Dr. Seymour, Paris.*
Banks of the Ru at Orgivaux (Seine-et-Oise) [Paris Exhibition, 1855].
Beach at Villerville (Salon, 1859), *Marseilles Museum.*
Beach at Villerville—Sunset (1873).
Brook in the Forest [Secrétan Coll.], *Mme. Isaac Périere, Paris.*
By the Side of the Pool, *A. Young, Esq., Blackheath.*
Chateau-Gaillard [Albert Wolff Coll.], *M. de Saint-Albin, Paris.*
Cooper's Shop, A (1872) [Morgan Coll., New York].
End of May [Stewart Coll., New York].
Ferry-boat, The (1858), *M. H. Lallemand, Paris.*
Ferryman of the Oise, *M. le Prince A. de Broglie.*
Fields in June, The (Salon, 1874).
Flock of Geese, *M. Mélot.*
Foot-bridge, The (1863), *M. F. Herz, Paris.*
Grey Morning on the Loire, *A. Young, Esq., Blackheath.*
Harvest (Salon, 1852).
House of "Mère Bazot" at Valmondois (where Daubigny lived) [Salon, 1874].
Island of Bezons (1850-51), *Avignon Museum.*
Landscape with River, Figures, and Cattle, *General H. Hopkinson, London.*

I

Mantes—Evening, *A. Young, Esq., Blackheath.*

Marsh, *Mrs. W. H. Vanderbilt, New York.*

Meadow at Valmandois [Paris Exhibition, 1855], *M. G. Claudon, Paris.*

Mid-day near a Pond [Albert Spencer Coll., New York].

Mill, The [des Gobelles] at Optevoz, 1857, *M. Georges Claudon, Paris.*

Moonlight, *J. Staat Forbes, Esq., London.*

Moonlight [Salon, 1865 ; Royal Academy, 1866], *H. T. Wells, Esq., R.A.*

Moonrise (Salon, 1861).

Moonrise [Salon, 1877].

Moonrise [Salon, 1868 ; Vienna Exhibition, 1873 ; Paris Exhibition, 1878].

Morning, *Mrs. W. H. Vanderbilt, New York.*

New Moon, The, *J. S. Forbes, Esq., London.*

On the Marne [Morgan Coll., New York].

On the Oise, *W. C. Quilter, Esq., M.P., London.*

On the Seashore, *J. S. Forbes, Esq., London.*

On the Seine [Morgan Coll., New York].

Orchard in Picardy (1862), *Mme. C. Aeloque, Paris.*

Orchard [Salon, 1876].

Pool, near Auvers [Laurent-Richard Coll.].

Pool near the Sea [Paris Exhibition, 1855].

Pool of Gylieu (1853). [Purchased by the Emperor Napoleon III.]

Poppy Field (1874), *P. H. Sears, Esq., Boston, U.S.*

Portijois, *Mme. Veuve J. Rœderer, Havre.*

Red Moon, The, *Mrs. S. D. Warren, Boston.*

Return of the Flock, 1877 [Secrétan Coll.], *G. A. Drummond, Esq., Montreal.*

Return of the Flock—Moonlight [Salon, 1859], *Boston Museum, U.S.*

Seascape, *Lyons Museum.*

Sea Piece, *M. Van den Eynde, Brussels.*

Sea Piece (small), *J. Agnew, Esq., Glasgow.*

Seine at Charenton, *Purchased by the Ministry of the Interior.*

Sheepfold (Salon, 1861).

Sluice in the Valley of Optevoz (Isère) [Paris Exhibition, 1855], *The Louvre.*

Sluice in the Valley of Optevoz, *Rouen Museum.*

Solitude (etched), *M. Raimbeaux.*

Spring [Salon, 1857], *The Louvre.*

St. Jerome in the Desert (Salon, 1840).

Stork's Retreat, The, *J. Staats Forbes, Esq., London.*

Summer Evening [Albert Spencer Coll., New York].

Summer Evening— On the Oise, *W. Thorburn, Esq., London.*

Sunrise (Banks of the Oise), *Lille Museum.*

Sunrise, *M. Oudinot, Boston, U.S.A.*

Sun Setting over the Sea, *The Hon. Mr. Justice Day, London.*

Town and River, with Bridge (Mantes), *J. Staat Forbes, Esq., London.*

Valley of the Arque, near Dieppe (1877), *M. Georges Kinen, Paris.*

Valley of Optevoz (small), [Salon, 1853], *M. Gilet.*

Valley of Optevoz (larger), [Salon, 1857. Purchased by the Emperor Napoleon III.].

View of Conflans (Junction of the Seine and Oise) [Defoer Coll.].

View of Dieppe (1877).

View on the Banks of the Seine, at Bezons (1852), *Nantes Museum.*

Village near Bonnières (Salon, 1861).

Village of Glouton, *M. Gustave Clodin.*

Village on the Banks of a River (1863) [J. Duncan Coll.], *M. H. Vever, Paris.*

Village on the Banks of the Oise—Sunset, *M. Ch. Leroux.*

Village on the Oise, *M. Roudillon, Paris.*

Villerville-sur-Mer [Salon, 1864], *Heer Mesdag, The Hague.*

Vintage (1863), *Louvre.*

Washerwoman, River Oullins, *Carcassonne Museum.*

Watercourse in a Meadow, *Mme. de Cassin, Paris.*

Windmills, Dordrecht [Salon, 1872], *Messrs. Arnold and Tripp, Paris.*

IX. ORIGINAL ETCHINGS BY DAUBIGNY.

A very complete list of Daubigny's etchings is given in the book by F. Henriet, " Charles Daubigny et son Œuvre gravé," and also in H. Beraldi's very useful work, " Les Graveurs du XIXme Siécle." They include some 117 different plates, mostly of a small size. Only the more important etchings are mentioned below :—

Le Printemps—*after his picture in the Louvre.*

Les Bergers sous Bois.

Parc à moutons—le matin.

Les Vendanges.

Le Gué.

" Cahiers d'Eaux-fortes," title, and 21 small etchings (Paris, 1851).

" Voyage en bateau, croquis à l'eau-forte," title, and 15 etchings.

Messrs. Boussod, Valadon, and Co. publish a series of 35 etchings by Daubigny.

Daubigny also illustrated a large number of books, including "Chants et Chanson populaires de la France": Curmer's "Pleïade" (Lai des deux amants—frontispiece).

Most of these book illustrations were made in early life, and were done in a careful and finished manner, very different from his later etchings, which are often very rough, sometimes mere impressions.

X. ETCHINGS, &C., AFTER PICTURES BY DAUBIGNY.

Solitude	Etched by	T. Chauvel.
Sunset	,,	Maxime Lalanne.
Moonrise	,,	,,
Village on the Oise	,,	G. Greux.
Twilight	,,	Walker.
Banks of the Oise		Photogravure.
Pond at Corbigny		Photogravure.

Vernier lithographed a series of twelve pictures by Daubigny.

Various smaller etchings, &c., have appeared in different sale catalogues and other publications. For a list of some of these see under "Etchings after Pictures and Drawings by Millet" in the volume on "Millet, Rousseau and Diaz."

DUPRÉ.

XI. BIBLIOGRAPHY.*

Claretie (Jules), "Jules Dupré" ("Peintres et Sculpteurs Contemporaines"—Artistes Vivants, pt. 8).
Montrosier (E.), "Jules Dupré" ("Les Artistes Modernes" No. 49).
"L'Art," 1875, V. 204 (by Jules Claretie). 1879, XVII. 311, XIX. 241 (by R. Ménard).
"L'Artiste," 1889, pp. 364 and 454 (by Camille Leymarie).
"Art Review," No. 1 (January, 1890, "Dupré," by Mrs. Henry Ady).
"Gazette des Beaux-Arts," 1873, VII. 190, "Collection Laurent-Richard," (by R. Ménard).

* See also the General Bibliography of the Painters of Barbizon in the companion volume of "Millet, Rousseau, and Diaz."

XII. SOME OF THE PRINCIPAL PAINTINGS BY DUPRÉ.

Animals Crossing a Bridge in Berry [Paris Exhibition, 1867; Edward Coll.].

At Sea, *W. T. Walters, Esq., Baltimore.*

Autumn Sunset, *Mrs. W. H. Vanderbilt, New York.*

Banks of a River (Secrétan Coll.), *Baron Alphonse de Rothschild, Paris.*

Bathers [Salon, 1839].

Battle of Hondschoote (the figures by Eugène Lami) [Salon, 1836], *Lille Museum.*

Boat at Sea : Stormy effect, *A. J. Kirkpatrick, Esq., Glasgow.*

Boat at Sea (nearly same as above), *J. Staat Forbes, Esq., London.*

Boats Stranded—Moonlight (Barque échoué—Claire de lune), *General H. Hopkinson, London.*

Bridge at Berry [Paris Exhibition, 1867].

Bright Day, *W. T. Walters, Esq., Baltimore.*

Brook, The, *Mrs. William Hooper, New York.*

Cows at the Drinking-place [Saulnier Coll.].

Cows Crossing a Ford, *Mme. Adolphe Moreau, Paris.*

Cows in a Pool, *J. H. Warren, Esq., New York.*

Deer in a Wood [S. Goldschmidt Coll.], *M. Basilewski, Paris.*

Entrance to a Village in the Landes [Salon, 1852].

Environs of Châteauroux [Salon, 1834].

Evening, 1867 [Prince Demidoff Coll.], *Luxembourg Gallery.*

Fishing Boat on the Open Sea [Faure and Laurent-Richard Colls.].

Flock of Sheep [Defoer Coll.].

Forest of Compiègne [Paris Exhibition, 1867].

Gorge of the " Eaux-Chaudes."

Hamlet in the Landes.

Harvest in Picardy (Salon, 1876).

Hay Cart [Wilson Coll.], *M. Leroux.*

Hay Waggon, *Miss C. L. Wolfe, New York.*

Homestead, The, *A. Young, Esq., Blackheath.*

Interior of a Farm House in Berry, 1833 [Faure Coll.].

In the Landes (1850), *M. Ferd. Herz, Paris.*

Landes, The [Laurent-Richard Coll.], *J. S. Forbes, Esq., London.*

Landscape with Cattle, *J. S. Forbes, Esq., London.*

Landscape with Cattle, *Holbrook Gaskell, Esq., Liverpool.*

Marsh, The, *M. Stumpf.*

Meadow, *Mrs. J. G. Fell, Philadelphia.*

Midday [Laurent-Richard Coll.], *Mrs. W. H. Vanderbilt, New York.*
Moonlight [Exposition Nationale, 1883], *M. Teste.*
Morass in the Basses-Pyrénées [Faure Coll.].
Morning, 1867 [Prince Demidoff Coll.], *Luxembourg Gallery.*
Morning [Morgan Coll.].
Normandy Meadow [Salon, 1884].
Old Oak, *W. T. Walters, Esq., Baltimore.*
Old Oak, *Miss C. L. Wolfe, New York.*
Overhanging Elm on the Oise [Laurent-Richard Coll.].
Pasturage at the Edge of the Forest, *M. F. Bischoffsheim, Paris.*
Pasturage [Salon, 1852].
Pastureland in Limousin [Salon, 1835 ; Paris Exhibition, 1889], *M. F.
    Bischoffsheim.*
Pond, The [Defoer Coll.].
Pool in La Sologne.
Pool in the Forest of Compiègne—Sunset, *Mme. la Baronne N. de Rothschild.*
Pool, The, *A. H. Talmadge, Esq.*
Pool, The (1854), *Dr. Jules Worms, Paris.*
Pool, The, *Mme. de Cassin, Paris.*
Promontory of the Downs ("Pointe des Dunes"), St. Quentin in the
    Manche (Seapiece) [Faure Coll.], *James Donald, Esq., Glasgow.*
Punt, The.
Return from Market [Laurent-Richard Coll.].
Return of the Flock [Paris Exhibition, 1867].
Return to the Farm—Sunset [J. Dupré Sale, 1890], *Duc d'Aumale.*
River-Pasturage on the Oise [Faure Coll.].
Road in the Landes.
Sand, Georges (Portrait).
Scene near Fontainebleau, *J. H. Warren, Esq., New York.*
Sea with Boat, *The Hon. Mr. Justice Day, London.*
Setting Sun [Salon, 1852].
Sheepfold in Berry [Paris Exhibition, 1867].
Shepherd, A [Faure Coll.].
Skirts of a Forest—A Storm [Faure Coll.].
Sluice (La Vanne) (painted about 1846), [Paris Exhibition, 1867], *late
    M. Van Praet's Coll., Brussels.*
Souvenir of the Landes.
Storm Effect, *M. Fraissinet, Marseilles.*
Sunset after a Storm, *M. J. C. Roux, Marseilles.*
Sunset [Defoer Coll.].

Symphony [Morgan Coll.].

Watercourse in Picardy.

Willows at Water's Edge, *M. Blancard.*

Willow Plantation [Van Praet and Wilson Colls.], *M. G. Lutz, Paris.*

Winding Road in the Forest of Compiègne.

Windmill [S. Goldschmidt Coll.], *M. Basilewski, Paris.*

View near Southampton [Salon, 1835 ; Paris Ex., 1889 ; Wilson Coll.], *M. J. Beer.*

XIII. ORIGINAL LITHOGRAPHS BY DUPRÉ.

Vue prise à Alençon.

Moulin de la Solonge.

Vue prise en Normandie.

Vue prise en Angleterre (Salon, 1836).

Bords de la Somme.

Pacage du Limousin.

Vue prise dans le Port de Plymouth.

All the above were originally published in some of the earlier volumes of "L'Artiste."

M. MAXIME LALANNE has made an important etching of the picture "MORNING," by Dupré, in the Luxembourg.

Various smaller etchings and lithographs have been made by the following artists : Marvy, Collingnon, Chauvel, Anastasi, François, Laurens, Mouilleron, Didier, Vernier, &c. A list of sale catalogues and other publications containing etchings, &c. after Dupré, will be found in the volume on "Millet, Rousseau, and Diaz" under "Etchings after Pictures and Drawings by Millet."

Copies of most of the etchings in the foregoing lists may be seen at Messrs. Obach & Co.'s, 20, Cockspur Street, London, W.

INDEX.

TO COROT.

	PAGE
About, Edmond . . .	28
Aligny . . . 8, 10, 11,	32
Baptism of Christ . . .	31
Bertin, Edouard . . .	10
Bertin, Victor . . . 7,	8
Biblis	25
Bodinier	10
"Bulletin de l'Ami des Arts"	28
Busson	5
Buttura	31
Cabat	28
Campagna of Rome . . 13,	21
Chenavard . . .	10
Chesneau, Ernest . . .	26
Clair de Lune, Le . .	24
Clément, Charles . . .	8
Clarétie, M. Jules . . 15, 16,	17
Coliseum, The . 10, 11, 13,	22
Courbet	9
Corot, Camille—	
1796, Born in Paris . . .	1
1806, Goes to school. . .	2
1812-1820, Employed by a draper	3
Acquaintance with Michalon . . .	3
Studies under . . .	6
Desires to become a painter . . .	5
His first study . .	5
Early influences . .	2
Moved to Ville d'Avray	2
Studies under Bertin .	7

	PAGE
Treatment in the Salon	13
His character . .	15
Description of him . .	16
Poetry of his art . .	17
Classic in style . .	9
1825-1827, Stay in Rome .	9
1827, Returns to France . .	13
Début in the Salon .	13
1833, Returns to Italy . .	21
1847, Receives the Legion of Honour . . .	22
1870, Generosity during the war	23
1874, Death of his sister . .	24
1874, Presentation of Gold Medal . . .	24
1875, His death . . .	25
Love of Music . .	30
His death, sale of his works . . .	13
His pupils . . .	30
Religious style . .	31
Daubigny	31
Delalain, M. . . .	3
Delacroix . . .	30
Democritus . . . 14,	31
Desbarrolles, M. . . .	14
Diana surprised at the Bath .	21
Dumesnil, M. 2, 5, 7, 10, 11,	13
Dupré	28
Father, Corot's . . .	1
Flight into Egypt . . .	31
Florence, from the Garden of the Grand Duke . . .	22
Flute Player . . .	14
Forum, The	13

	PAGE
Fournel, M.	4
Français . . . 5, 30
Fromentin . . . 26
Géricault . . . 7, 8
Graham, Mr. Stevens . . 17
Great Grandfather, Corot's . 2
Guérin, Pierre . . 10
Hagar . . . 14, 31
Hanoteau, M. . . 11
Huet, Paul . . . 8
Jérôme, St. . . . 31
Jolivard . . . 28
Lake of Némi . . 4
Lenormant, M. . . 26
Little Apple Gatherers . 14
Marilhat . . . 28
Ménard, M. René . 3, 6
Michalon . . 3, 6, 8
Monk, A . . . 31
Morning . . . 4
Mother, Corot's . . 1
Musset, Alfred de . 21
Nymphs at the Bath . 14
Planche, M. Gustave . . 26

	PAGE
Pleasures of Evening, The . 25
Poussin . . . 32
Rembrandt . . . 32
Robaut, Alfred . . 13
Robert, Léopold . . 10
Rome, from the Campo Vaccina 22
Rousseau, M. J. . . 10
Rousseau, Théodore . . 28
Schnetz . . . 10
Silvestre . . 1, 9, 11, 21, 22
Sister, Corot's elder . . 1
Sister, Corot's younger . . 1
Soir, Le . . . 24
Souvenir d'Arleux . . 24
Timbal, M. Charles . . 4, 26
Titian . . . 32
Troyon . . . 5
Volcanic Lands near Marina, The . . . 22
Volterra . . . 22
View taken at Narni . 13
View of the Grand Canal . 12
View of the Tyrol . . 14
Vue Générale (of Genoa) . 22
Wolff, Albert . . 15, 16

TO DAUBIGNY.

	PAGE
About, Edmond . . 48
Adam and Eve . . 44
Angling . . . 57
Apollo tending Sheep . 44
Appian, Adolphe . . 50
Aubry, d' . . . 36
Aunt, Daubigny's . . 36
Banks of the Oise . . 52
Barbizon Painters . . 46
Bazot, Mme. . . 37
Bertin, Victor . . 35

	PAGE
Bord de l'Oise . . 55
Bourdin, Ernest . . 54
Busson, Charles . . 53
Chintreuil . . . 58
Clément de Ris, Comte . 50
Corot . . 45, 49, 56, 58
Curmer . . . 54
Dautel, Henriette Virginie 36, 38
Daliphart . . . 58
Delaroche, Paul . 44, 45

	PAGE
Daumier	56
Delloze	54
Dechaume, Geoffroy .	41, 42
Desgoffe, M. . . .	48
Diaz	46
Dupré	46
Daubigny—	
1817, Born in Paris . .	35
His early years . .	36
Left home . .	37
Exhibiting at the Salon	38
Walks to Italy .	39
His companions .	42
1840, Studies etching .	43
Competes for the Prix de Rome	44
Engraver and painter .	44
1841, Fails for the Prix de Rome	44
A realist . .	47
Founder of a school .	53
1841 and 1845, Exhibits etchings in Salon . .	54
1857, Receives Legion of Honour . .	58
1861, Change in style .	58
1866, Tour in England .	55
1871, Journey to Holland .	55
1868, Journey to Spain .	55
1859, Builds "Le Botin" .	55
1868, Builds a house at Auvers	55
Visits Florence, Rome, and Naples . .	39
Walks back to Paris .	40
Obtains employment .	40
Visits Holland .	41
1874, Promoted to be Officier .	58
1878, His death . .	58
Father, Daubigny's . .	35
Fouzère . . .	38
Furne	54
Géricault . . .	46
Grandmother, Daubigny's .	36
Granet	40
Groizeillez . . .	58
Hachette . . .	54
Harvest . . .	49
Henriet, M. 36, 38, 42, 43, 44, 46, 52, 54, 55, 58	
Herpin	58
Hetzel	54
House at Auvers . . .	56
Huet, Paul . . .	46
Ile Saint-Louis . . .	42
Lake of Gylien . .	49, 50
Lambinet, Emile . .	53
Laneue, Hippolyte .	44
Lavieille, Eugène . .	53
Leroux, Charles . .	53
Lever du Soleil, Le . .	57
Loch Gate in the Valley of Opteroz	52
Meyer, Dr. Julius 45, 46, 49, 50, 52	
Meissonier . .	35, 38
Mignon . .	39, 40
Millet . . .	41, 58
"Monde Illustré, Le" .	56
Moine, La . . .	42
Oudinot . . .	56
Jérôme in the Desert, St.	37, 43
Parc à Moutons, Le .	57
Pelloquet, M. Théodore .	47
Poussin . . .	48
Rembrandt . . .	35
Rousseau . . . 45, 46, 58	
Spring . . . 48, 52, 58	
Steinheil . . .	42
Tonnelle, La . . .	42
Trimolet . . 42, 43	
Uncle, Daubigny's . .	36
Valley of Opteroz . .	58
View of the Banks of the Seine	49
View of the Chevet, A .	42
Villerville-sur-Mer .	58
Villeville, Léon .	53
Voilà la Campagne . .	48
Yriarte, M. Charles . .	56

TO DUPRE

	PAGE
Aligny	74
André, Jules . . 67, 68
Barbizon School . . 73
Barye . . . 67, 70
Battle Scene . . . 68
Bertin, Victor . . 69
Bidault 69
Bonington . . 61, 62
Boulanger, Louis . . 71
Brother, Dupre's . . 64
Cabat, Louis 62, 63, 65, 66, 68, 74, 75
Chenavard . . . 70
Chesneau, M. Ernest . 59, 60
Colin 67
Constable . . 61, 62
Corot . . . 59, 61, 74
Côtes de Granville . . 67
Clarétie 61
Clément, Charles . . 65
Daubigny . . 60, 62, 65, 73
Décamps . . 67, 70, 71, 74
Delaberge 74
Delacroix, Eugène . 67, 70
Delécluze, M. . . . 60
Deveria 67
Diaz . 65, 66, 67, 68, 71, 74
Diébold 64
Dujardin, Karel . . 66, 68
Dupré—
1812, Born in Paris . . 63
Follows his father's calling . . 64
Early education shortened . . 64
Works under Diébold . 64
Early life . . . 66
Teacher of Rousseau . 61
1831, Début in the Salon . 67
Description of work . 19
Part of his youth in England . . 68
1833, Invites Rousseau to travel with him . . 70

	PAGE
1840, Entertains at his lodgings . . . 70
Returns to Monsoult . 70
1843, Travels with Rousseau in Gascony . . 70
Kindness to Rousseau . 71
1848, Receives Legion of Honour . . . 71
Retires from public life . 71
1852, Takes up his work again 71
Alteration of style . . 72
His character . . . 67
Choice of scenes . . 73
Retires to Cayeux . . 74
Goes to Barbizon . . 74
1889, His death . . . 74
Dusigneur, Jehan . . 71
Eté en Voyage, Un . . 74
Father, Dupre's . . . 63
Faust 67
Flandrin, Paul . . . 59
Flers, Camille . 62, 66, 67, 68
Français, Louis . 59, 74
Fuseli 61
Garbet 71
Géricault . . . 61
Gigoux 71
Giroux 75
Haussard 61
Huet, Paul . . 62, 68, 75
Huysman 69
Interior of a Forest . . 69
Jadin 68
Jameson, Mrs. . . . 61
Jeanron 67
Johannot 67
Jolivet 75
Laberge, Charles . . 62
Landon 71
Lami, Eugène . . 67, 68
Lanoue, Hippolyte . . 59

	PAGE
Laviron	71
Lenormant, M. . . .	67
Liberty	67
Limousin	69
Littré	60
Lorentz	71
Luebke	59
Passage of Animals over a Bridge . . .	72
Planché, M. . . .	71
Poussin	66
Poterlet	67
Préault	71
Mantz, Paul . . 62, 72
Marilhat	68
Marvy, Louis . . .	74
Ménard, M. René, 64, 65, 66, 67, 74
Meyer	74
Michallon . . 61, 69,

	PAGE
Regnier	75
Ricourt	71
Rousseau, Théodore 60, 67, 69, 70, 72, 74
Roquelin	67
Roqueplan	68
Ruysdael	69
Scheffer, Ary . . 67, 70
Sensier, M. Alfred . 67, 69, 70
Sunset	62
Thoré . . . 68, 71
Troyon	62
Turner	62
Valenciennes . . .	69
Vanne, La . . .	72
Vue d'Angleterre . .	68
Wolff, M. Albert . . 60, 61

TO CONCLUSION.

	PAGE
Antigna	92
Bacler d'Albe . . .	81
Barbizon School . . .	90
Baudry, Paul . . .	96
Boisselier, Felix . .	81
Belmont, Louise Sarrazin de.	81
Berchem	82
Bequignot	81
Bertin, Jean Victor . .	80
Bidault, Xavier . .	80
Boucher	79
Bonington . . 90, 91, 97
Bonnefond	94
Boquet, Didier . .	81
Bourgeois, Amédée . .	81
Bruandet	80
Breton, Jules-Adolphe .	96
Cabat, Louis . . .	99
Cascades of Tivoli . .	82
Caraud	97
Constable, John . .	98

	PAGE
Chasseur of the Imperial Guards . . .	84
Champmartin . . .	84
Caravaggio . . .	84
Chardin	95
Chesneau . . . 84, 85
Claude	79
Cogniet	84
Comte	97
Correggio	83
Corot	81
Courbet . . . 95, 96
Couture	96
Crissé, Turpin de . .	81
Dante and Virgil . .	85
David . 77, 80, 83, 84, 92
Décamps . . 89, 90, 96
Delaborde	81
Delacroix, Eugène 84, 85, 89, 98
Delaroche . . . 91, 94
Demarne, Louis . .	82

	PAGE
Diaz 90, 96, 99	
Dunouy 81	
Dupont, Pierre . . . 96	
Dupré 99	
Everdingen 82	
Flers, Camille . . . 99	
Frère, Ed. 92	
Fromentin . . . 97	
Gendron 92	
Géricault . 77, 78, 83, 84, 85, 87, 88, 89, 95	
Gérôme . . . 92, 97	
Grobon, Michel . . . 83	
Guérin. . . . 84, 90	
Hamman 97	
Hamon 92	
Hebert. . . . 92, 94	
Hédouin, Edmond . . . 92	
Hillemacher 97	
Hooch, Peter de . . . 90	
Huet, Paul 99	
Hugo, Victor . . . 85	
Idealists, the . . . 85, 88	
Ingres . . 85, 87, 88, 91, 94, 96	
Isabey, Eugène . . . 91, 98	
Jeanrat 95	
Jelabert 92	
Jolivard, André . . . 83	
Laberge, Charles de . . . 99	
Landelle 92	
Lake of Nemi . . . 82	
Landscape painting . . . 78	
Lantara 80	
Lehmann, Rodolph . . . 94	
Lemaître, Frédéric . . . 85	
Leman 97	
Lancret 80	
Le Nain 95	

	PAGE
Leonardo 83	
Maas, Nicolaas . . . 90	
Malaria, The . . . 94	
Meissoni-r . . . 97	
Meyer. Herr . 78, 80, 82, 94	
Michallon, Achille . . 81	
Millet . . . 93, 96	
Müller, Carl . . . 94	
Musset, Alfred de . . . 85	
Pater 79	
Pignerolle, Charles de . . 94	
Poussin . . . 79, 81	
Prud'hon . . . 83, 84	
Raphael . . . 84, 88	
Realism 97	
Rembrandt . . 79, 84, 90	
Robert, Hubert . . . 80	
Robert, Léopold . . 92, 94	
Raft of the Medusa . . 84, 88	
Romantic School . . . 84	
Roqueplan, Camille . . 91, 99	
Rousseau 99	
Rubens 84	
Ruysdael . . . 80, 82	
Sand, Georges . . . 96	
Scheffer, Ary . 84, 89, 90	
Schnetz 94	
Thoré 88	
Titian 84	
Valenciennes, Henri . 80, 81, 82	
Vernet, Carl . . . 84	
Vernet, Joseph . . . 80	
Vischer 79	
Watelet, Louis Etienne 82, 83	
Watteau . . . 79, 89	
Wounded Cuirassier . . 84	

PRINTED BY J. S. VIRTUE AND CO., LIMITED, CITY ROAD, LONDON.

Printed in the United States
141446LV00002BA/92/A